THE GOOD, THE BAD & THE UNLIKELY

THE GOOD, THE BAD & the UNLIKELY

AUSTRALIA'S PRIME MINISTERS

MUNGO MacCALLUM

Published by Black Inc.,
an imprint of Schwartz Media Pty Ltd
37–39 Langridge Street
Collingwood VIC 3066 Australia
email: enquiries@blackincbooks.com
http://www.blackincbooks.com

The National Library of Australia Cataloguing-in-Publication entry:

MacCallum, Mungo, 1941–

The good, the bad and the unlikely : Australia's prime ministers / Mungo MacCallum.

ISBN: 9781863955539 (pbk.)

Prime ministers—Australia. Australia—Politics and government.

994.0099

CONTENTS

Introduction
1
Edmund Barton
5
Alfred Deakin
16
John Christian Watson
26
George Houstoun Reid
31
Andrew Fisher
37
Joseph Cook
45
William Morris Hughes
50
Stanley Melbourne Bruce
60
James Henry Scullin
66
Joseph Aloysius Lyons
74
Earle Christmas Grafton Page
80
Robert Gordon Menzies
85
Arthur William Fadden
97

John Joseph Curtin
101
Francis Michael Forde
111
Joseph Benedict Chifley
115
Harold Edward Holt
125
John McEwen
131
John Grey Gorton
136
William McMahon
145
Edward Gough Whitlam
150
John Malcolm Fraser
161
Robert James Lee Hawke
169
Paul John Keating
178
John Winston Howard
187
Kevin Michael Rudd
199
Julia Eileen Gillard
206
Note on Sources
213

INTRODUCTION

Australians aren't very fond of their politicians, alive or dead; we have raised no great monuments to our former leaders.

We have no Lincoln Memorial, let alone a Mount Rushmore. But in the Victorian city of Ballarat, which has the distinction of being represented by two prime ministers – Alfred Deakin and James Scullin – there is an exception.

In the well-kept Botanic Gardens, near the lake, is the Prime Ministers Avenue: a double row of bronze busts of our heads of government from federation to the present day. These are the brainchild and gift of Richard Crouch, who had the distinction of being the youngest member of the parliament of 1901 and, coincidentally, served at different times under both Deakin and Scullin. A noted patron of the arts, Crouch commissioned the first six busts in the avenue and left a bequest to enable the project to continue indefinitely; which it has.

Today, the first thing that strikes the visitor is the sheer number; for a country that has only recently passed its first centenary as a nation, we seem to have had more Prime Ministers than strictly necessary. The impression is compounded by the recollection that just one of them, Robert Menzies, had a total of nineteen years, and another two, Bob Hawke and John Howard, about the same between them. It doesn't leave a lot to be divided among the other two dozen. Perhaps the speed of the turnover reflects the dynamism of a young, bustling country, or perhaps Australians just have a short attention span. But it has given us a parade of leaders which is pretty impressive – at least in bronze.

At the top of the avenue are the founding fathers, Edmund Barton and Alfred Deakin; then we work our way through the other early federationists, Chris Watson and George Reid, and into the war years with Andrew Fisher, Joseph Cook and Billy Hughes. Stanley Bruce takes us to the Depression and Jimmy Scullin into it. Joseph Lyons and Earle Page complete the lead-up to World War II, and Robert Menzies, Arthur Fadden and John Curtin take us through it. Frank Forde and Ben Chifley usher us out of it and into the second Menzies era; then there is the flurry of Menzies's successors – Harold Holt, John McEwen, John Gorton and Billy McMahon – before modern times begin with Gough Whitlam, Malcolm Fraser, Bob Hawke and Paul Keating. The two bespectacled dumplings of John Howard and Kevin Rudd provide a rather anti-climactic finish – in the spring of 2011 Julia Gillard's bust, like her prime ministership, was still a work in progress.

As a more personal indication of the rate of change, I note that my own lifetime spans fifteen of the figures – more than half – and that I have known twelve of them and been on first-name terms with eleven. I offer this as my credential for presuming to write about them in less than worshipful tones – that and my lifelong fascination with the political process. Even in its darkest phases (and it must be admitted that recent times have not been all that bright) it remains our only hope; as a wise man once said, it is the only way we can resolve our disputes without killing each other.

And it should be said that all those who have led us – yes, all – have in their own way kept that great ideal in mind. Of course, some have done better than others; among the number have been successes and failures and mere seat-warmers – the good, the bad and the unlikely. But in all of them I have found something I can relate to, something that is recognisably part of the Australia to which they have led us.

Doing the research has also led me to a bit of rethinking. I found the revered but many-faced Deakin a far less admirable character than I had expected, and I discovered a lot to like about Reid, often dismissed as a buffoon. I unearthed redeeming features in Hughes, the great Labor rat, but not many in Page, celebrated as the first doyen of the Country Party. I was surprised by the number of flaws in Curtin, although these were reduced to insignificance by his achievements, and I ended up wondering if Chifley, perhaps the most loved of our leaders, was really up to the job.

Reviewing my contemporaries was harder; it is difficult to be objective about people you think you know. But I was confirmed in my belief that the most significant were the most courageous, the ones who burst through the roadblocks not only in society but within their own parties.

Gorton attacked the shibboleth of states' rights to which the Liberals had clung long after it had become a hindrance to good government; he took on the conservative premiers from around the country and, in the process, saved the Great Barrier Reef from oil drilling. Whitlam turned the Labor Party upside down, trashing White Australia and the sectarian opposition to state aid, and, it is often forgotten, started the breakdown of tariff barriers and the whole system of protection. Keating completed the process by floating the currency and opening up the financial networks to international competition. These were the heroes, the ones who chose, in Whitlam's phrase, to crash through or crash; in the end they did both. None of them lasted much longer than a single term in office.

As I said, Australians aren't very fond of their politicians. Perhaps we would appreciate them better if we knew more about them. Now, read on.

EDMUND BARTON

A FEW YEARS ago not very many Australians had ever heard of Edmund Barton. Now, thanks to an advertising campaign about something else entirely, most can name our first Prime Minister.

But that's about where it begins and ends. Few, if any, could pick him out of a line-up of the founding fathers, the group of ambitious and hirsute politicians who brought about the federation of the fractious colonies and gave us the constitution and form of government we enjoy (or don't) today. One easy way to single out Barton was to look for the sole clean-shaven face.

Like most of their descendants, this motley bunch was driven by a combination of idealism and self-interest, and getting them to agree on anything substantial was like herding a football team into a temperance meeting. It was Barton's peculiar genius that he was able to convince not only the politicians, but also the populace at large, that it was time to make, in his only memorable line, "for the first time in history … a nation for a continent and a continent for a nation" and then to demonstrate that the resulting national government could actually work.

On the face of it he seemed an unlikely candidate for a political role. The youngest of eleven children of one of Sydney's first stockbrokers, Edmund Barton was born in Glebe, a Sydney suburb, in 1849. His mother ran a private girls' school and by all accounts the family was a literary one. Edmund, nicknamed Toby, was certainly of that inclination and after passing through Fort Street Model School and Sydney Grammar (where he was school captain) studied classics at Sydney University.

His talent for mediation showed itself early. A keen cricketer, he was umpiring a match between New South Wales and Lord Harris's English XI when an altercation between players turned into a full-scale riot; Barton managed to calm things down, and was recognised by keen judges as a budding politician. His schoolfriend Richard O'Connor, who was already set on that course, had encouraged him to try debating at the Sydney Mechanics' School of Arts, and although Barton never became a great orator, he learned how to mount a convincing argument. After working for three years in legal offices in Sydney he was admitted to the bar in 1871.

But he was already showing a preference for the other kind of bar. He became a habitué of Sydney's Athenaeum Club, the haunt of the literati and other dilettantes including the founding editor of the *Bulletin*, J.F. Archibald. It seemed something of a stab in the back when Archibald's magazine christened Barton "Tosspot Toby" – a nickname that stuck for life.

When he finally entered politics, it seemed more for want of something better to do than through any burning ambition. He stood for the Sydney University seat in the NSW Legislative Assembly in 1876 and again in 1877, losing both times; he eventually won it in 1879. Next year he transferred to the seat of Wellington, and in 1882 to East Sydney – in those days electoral loyalty was not seen as a prerequisite. The dominant political philosophy in New South Wales was free trade, as opposed to Victoria's protectionism; more through convenience than conviction Barton announced himself as a free trader, and in 1883 was rewarded with the speakership.

It was a role tailor-made for him; then as now the state parliament was a bear pit and physical brawling during the late night sessions was not uncommon. Barton again proved his skill in quelling riots and restoring calm, even if he did have to expel some of the more unruly members to demonstrate his resolve. He was marked as a coming man by his seniors, and was offered the post of Attorney-General by Premier Sir George Dibbs, but the coming man refused to come; Barton preferred the comfort of the speakership, not to mention the fact that it paid £1200 a year – more than he had ever been able to make at the bar.

In 1887 he resigned that post and moved to the loftier climes of Legislative Council, where so many political careers have drifted away in inebriated torpor. Given Barton's apparent lack of ambition to date, his might have been expected to do the same. But in 1889 something else happened, which galvanised the nation, and Edmund Barton with it: New South Wales Premier Sir Henry Parkes made a speech in the town of Tenterfield on the need for the colonies to federate.

The idea itself was not new; it had even been discussed at the Athenaeum Club. But it needed an advocate of Parkes's calibre to turn it into a cause. Barton read the Tenterfield speech then attended a meeting at Sydney Town Hall at which Parkes put his case to an enthusiastic crowd, and he was hooked. In his own words, federation was "the one big idea", and he dedicated himself to bringing it about, initially as Parkes's apostle and later as his chosen successor, as leader of the campaign.

The first step was the national convention of 1891. An outline for a federal constitution had been drawn up by Barton's fellow Athenaeum Club member Andrew Inglis Clark, but it was far too radical for most of the delegates. They were, after all, representatives of the colonial parliaments, politicians eager to safeguard their own rights and privileges. They were naturally reluctant to cede any more of their existing powers to a putative central government than was absolutely unavoidable, and concessions would have to be prised out of them.

Barton set himself to do the prising. He took it as a given that once the colonies became states in a federation, trade between them would be free; but as sop to the protectionists he insisted that their "territorial rights", a happily undefined concept, should be preserved. The colonies were relying on the powers of the proposed upper house, the states' house, to defend them against the popularly elected lower house; they wanted absolute equality and the power of an outright veto. Barton secured the vital compromise: the upper house would be able to reject legislation proposed by the lower house, but it would not be able to amend money bills. As 1975 showed, this would not prevent critical conflict between the two houses, but it did make it less likely.

Barton's efforts drew him to the attention of the heavyweights in the federation movement; Alfred Deakin and Sir John Downer pronounced themselves impressed, and when Clark had to resign from the drafting committee for health reasons, Barton joined Queensland's Sir Samuel Griffith and South Australia's Charles Kingston in the task of writing the new constitution.

But he set himself another equally onerous goal. As the oldest, largest and most assertive of the colonies, New South Wales was arguably the one with the most to lose through federation – at least a number of politicians saw it that way, among them George Reid, the new leader of the Free Trade Party. For Barton, the cause of federation now transcended old party loyalties. He resigned from the Legislative Council, stood against Reid in his old seat of East Sydney and topped the poll. Barton was now the acknowledged leader of the federal movement in New South Wales and the ageing Parkes persuaded him to accept the title officially when his government fell later that year.

The protectionist George Dibbs became Premier and, to the surprise of many, offered Barton the post of Attorney-General. Even more to their surprise, Barton accepted; he felt that only by working inside the tent could he get the draft constitution accepted by the NSW parliament. But despite his best efforts the bill was jammed in the committee stages. At the same time he put the labour movement offside by sending police in against striking miners in Broken Hill. The last straw was a perceived conflict between his private legal practice and his role as the colony's first law officer. Worn out, broke and generally disillusioned he resigned in 1893 and had a big drink. His enemies gloated that his career was over.

But for Barton himself, 1894 was just another opportunity for change. Having failed to be re-elected, this time in the seat of Randwick, he took his campaign to the people. For three years he stumped the colony, addressing some 300 meetings. In the process he gathered a band of young disciples including Robert Garran, who played the part of Peter to Barton's Messiah; the analogy is apt because although the campaign was ostensibly about promoting federation it also served to elevate Barton to hitherto unimagined heights of popularity. By a fortunate coincidence, those in charge of the formal campaign had also decided that the cause should be returned to the people, and so delegates to the 1897 convention were not chosen by the parliaments but elected by popular vote. Barton headed the poll by a wide margin: he was acknowledged as the leader of the movement and became chairman of the national convention and of its vital drafting and constitutional committees.

After an adjournment during which the NSW parliament tried once again to scuttle the draft constitution bill (there were so many amendments Barton complained: "you might as well say you would improve a horse by cutting his legs off"), the convention resumed in 1898 and the bill was finally sent to a referendum in June of that year. The conservative opposition, led as always by the business community and the *Daily Telegraph*, forced through a provision that to be carried, the bill would need not only a majority, but a minimum of 80,000 "yes" votes; their campaign ensured that it fell well short of the figure. Barton once more became the great conciliator. Re-elected as a member of the Legislative Assembly, he became leader of the opposition and at first clashed bitterly with the Premier, George Reid, who was at best equivocal about federation. But Reid sought and won concessions from Barton, and eventually the two campaigned together for a second referendum. On 29 June 1899 the draft constitution bill was approved by a big margin – 107,420 in favour to 82,741 against.

The next step was to persuade the colony's masters in Whitehall to accept it; to become valid the bill needed to be passed as an act of the Westminster parliament. Accompanied by Alfred Deakin and Charles Kingston, Barton set out for London, where his persuasive powers would be put to their sternest test. The sticking point was the Privy Council. Barton wanted its power to hear appeals from Australian courts abolished, leaving the forthcoming High Court of Australia as the nation's ultimate arbiter. The British colonial secretary Joseph Chamberlain insisted that the appeal system must stay. Barton eventually brokered a compromise: while for most cases the right of appeal to the Privy Council would remain, in all cases involving the Australian constitution, the High Court would be the end of the line. When the deal was struck the British left the room, and the Australians celebrated, as Deakin's diary records: "When the door closed upon us and left us alone, we seized each other's hands and danced hand in hand in a ring around the centre of the room to express our jubilation!"

Barton was now the obvious candidate for the job of first Prime Minister, although his opponents were still expressing doubts about his temperament and his drinking. But the final barrier was not his personal habits, but protocol. The newly arrived Governor-General, Lord Hopetoun, felt compelled to make the first offer to the senior Premier of the time – Sir William Lyne of New South Wales. The trouble was that Lyne had been a vocal opponent of federation. It was therefore believed that he would, in all conscience, refuse the appointment; but in fact he snapped it up. Deakin, appalled, hit the telegraph office and quickly persuaded two other premiers, George Turner from Victoria and Frederick Holder from South Australia, to refuse to serve under Lyne. It quickly became obvious that Lyne could not form any kind of representative cabinet, and he pulled out. Hopetoun commissioned Barton; it was Christmas Eve 1900, an auspicious date by any measure. Federation's Messiah was finally anointed.

Barton's first cabinet was an all-star line-up: the premiers, including Lyne, were all there, along with Deakin and Kingston and Barton's old friend Richard O'Connor. These last three quickly became Barton's kitchen cabinet; to balance Kingston's radicalism, the Western Australian conservative Sir John Forrest was sometimes asked to join them. Together they made a disparate, fiery and highly ambitious collection; Barton's skills as a chairman and moderator were frequently tested. He described his government as protectionist, and the opposition was led by the free trader George Reid. The two parties went to the 1901 election under these labels, but neither could win a majority: Barton ended up controlling 32 seats and Reid 26, with the Australian Labor Party (ALP) holding the balance of power with the remaining 17. In the Senate Barton's position was even more precarious: he secured a mere 11 to Reid's 17, with the Labor Party on eight.

Deakin and Kingston set out to woo Labor's leader Chris Watson. It was not easy: the Labor Party had never forgiven Barton for breaking the Broken Hill strike, a confrontation which resulted in the jailing of several union leaders. Watson demanded, as the price of his support, legislation to enable the new government to take control of industrial relations, and the immediate implementation of the White Australia policy. Neither project presented any great ideological difficulty; Deakin and Kingston in particular were enthusiasts for a Commonwealth conciliation and arbitration commission, and at the turn of the century White Australia was a given.

Modern apologists such as Keith Windshuttle have tried to whitewash this policy (if one can use the phrase) by claiming that it was actually about keeping out cheap labour and not about race at all. This is simply not true. Here is Barton himself on the subject: "I do not think that the doctrine of the equality of man was ever intended to include racial equality ... these races are, in comparison with the white races – I think no one wants convincing of this fact – unequal and inferior." Implementing the policy, however, was problematic. There were two parts to it: banning the entry of non-whites, including Britain's allies, the Japanese; and getting rid of the ones already here, principally the kidnapped Kanakas who supplied free labour for the Queensland sugarcane fields. The second was solved by subsidies, tariffs and other handouts for the sugar growers, and the first through a lot of serious diplomacy; in the end Barton was rewarded with Japan's Order of the Rising Sun.

As a protectionist, Barton set up a wide-ranging system of tariffs, which not only satisfied the ideological bent of his followers but also provided his government with a handy source of revenue – sorely needed in the days before income tax. He paid close attention to setting up the Commonwealth public service, emphasising the need for quality, integrity and independence. He negotiated a naval agreement with Britain, sent a contingent of Australian troops to the Boer War and drafted the framework for a national railway system. It was a frenetic period, marked by his return to the bottle.

It was all too much for the proprietor of *Truth*, John Norton, himself a drinker of Olympic standard. In one of his frequent forays into politics Norton published a diatribe: "I charge you with being very frequently under the influence of drink ever since the meeting of the federal parliament ... and when you were supposed to be discharging the duties of your high constitutional office of Prime Minister … Quite recently you came into chamber so drunk you were scarcely able to stand ... on another occasion, seeing your drunken, helpless state, the Speaker generously put an end to the painful scene [when] he saw you were incapable of properly doing [so]…"

Unsurprisingly Barton relapsed into depression at the beginning of 1902.

The cure proved to be a trip to Britain during which he became a Knight Grand Cross of the Order of St Michael and St George – the highest rank then available to a colonial – a free citizen of Edinburgh, an honorary bencher at Gray's Inn and an honorary doctor of Oxford (to add to the Cambridge doctorate received on his first trip). On the way home he collected a medallion from the Pope. But all the gongs in the world could not save his leadership. The establishment of the arbitration commission was proving intractable: he was unable to balance the demands of the Labor Party with those of his own followers. In July 1903 Kingston, who had charge of the bill, resigned and two months later Barton followed him.

He immediately took up a position as senior puisne judge of the newly formed High Court under his old colleague Chief Justice Sir Samuel Griffith and alongside his old friend and equally keen fisherman Richard O'Connor. He was eminently suited to the job; even as a practising politician his real talents had often been more judicial than adversarial, and on the bench he could indulge them to the full. As the young Robert Menzies, never one to bestow praise lightly, put it: "A rich and beautifully modulated voice, a handsome and dignified appearance, exquisite courtesy, embracing both deference to his colleagues and genuine consideration for counsel, a clear sense of relevancy, a scholarly diction; all these things Barton possessed and practised. Taken singly, they are not commonplace; in combination, they marked Barton out for distinction."

He remained a devoted family man, taking his wife Jeannie and family to Tasmania for holidays, and then to Britain where he was, ironically enough, appointed to the Privy Council. It was the last of his many honours; he died suddenly of a heart attack in January 1920 and, after a state funeral, was buried at South Head cemetery.

Much of Barton's legacy now appears out of date; we have dispensed with White Australia and torn down most of the tariff wall. But it is not for his legislation that he should be remembered. His real, his unparalleled legacy was to bring the bickering colonies to federation, and then, as our first Prime Minister, to show that it could be made to work. It is an achievement that makes the so-called great reforms trumpeted by modern politicians look very petty indeed.

ALFRED DEAKIN

IF HENRY PARKES was the father of federation and Edmund Barton its midwife, then Alfred Deakin was its nanny. It was Deakin, as the outstanding politician of the first decade of the Commonwealth, who nursed the fractious infant through its childhood illnesses, checked its tantrums and set it on the path to a sturdy adolescence.

Deakin considered himself the true leader of the federation movement; he despised Parkes as a bully and a show-off, and considered Barton to be a lazy drunk. But he recognised that they had one thing he could never aspire to: they came from New South Wales. New South Wales was not only the first colony, it remained the biggest and most bumptious; and of the major settlements, it was the one most suspicious of federation. It was clear from the beginning that the Cornstalks would join the movement only if it was led by one of their own, so Deakin, with all the grace he could muster, deferred to those he considered his inferiors.

There is little doubt that his assessment was accurate: the

suave and handsome Melburnian was the greater intellect, the more compelling orator and the more visionary statesman; Robert Menzies, not the most self-effacing of judges, ranked Deakin as the best Prime Minister Australia had produced. But he also had his weaknesses. Although "Affable Alfred", as he was known from his youth, was an easygoing conversationalist, a man at home in most social situations, he never quite mastered the common touch and as a result never achieved the mass following that Barton did. Even in his own colony of Victoria, where he was something of a home-town hero, he was regarded with admiration and even awe, but not with affection.

This lack of popular appeal in no way diminished his achievements but it did mean that, unlike Barton, he could not rely on unquestioned public support to see him through the difficult political times; and in those early days, most of the political times were not just difficult, but bloody close to insoluble. Deakin, who might have expected a long unbroken run as Prime Minister, actually served three truncated terms, and was finally heaved unceremoniously into the political wilderness. Such, he might have mused, is fate.

Alfred Deakin was born in Fitzroy in 1856, the son of a tradesman who had risen to become a manager of Cobb and Co., the intercolonial transport consortium. He was educated at Melbourne Grammar, where he was considered talented but a bit of a dreamer, and, like Barton, drifted into law. He enrolled at Melbourne University, but like many students spent more time on his extracurricular interests, one of which was the debating club.

His real passion was spiritualism. From 1869 to 1870 he gave lessons on the subject to the Melbourne Progressive

Spiritualist Lyceum, and in 1875 gave a series of "trance" lectures for a publication known as "The Harbringer (sic) of Light" Then in 1877 he published a work entitled *The New Pilgrim's Progress*, which he said had been dictated to him by the spirit of John Bunyan himself. Bunyan was not his only tutor on the other side; when Deakin went into politics a couple of years later, he claimed to be receiving instruction from the ghosts of Sophocles, John Knox, Lord Macaulay, Edmund Burke, John Stuart Mill and (rather out of place in such exalted company) a former Victorian chief secretary named Richard Heales.

His introduction to the real world of politics came from a more earthly source: the Liberal editor of the Melbourne *Age*, David Syme. After an introduction in 1878, Syme took Deakin, who had understandably failed to pick up many legal briefs, under his wing as a special writer. This was his start in journalism, a craft which stood him in good stead on many future occasions. But Syme also recruited his young protégé to the protectionist cause, and found him a seat in the Victorian Legislative Assembly. The latter process was a kerfuffle; in 1879 Deakin narrowly won West Bourke, but resigned because of irregularities in the poll. He lost the rerun, and lost again in the general election of 1880, but finally won the seat when the government fell later that year.

He quickly proved an adept negotiator, a backroom operator who understood the vital art of compromise, and he was rewarded with a series of ministries between 1883 and 1890, including a stretch as Premier. He did impressive work in the fields of irrigation, bringing water into public ownership, and industrial relations; his Factories and Shops Act put limits on the hours women and children could be made to work, and introduced the idea of workers compensation.

But his big moment came when he led the Victorian delegation to the colonial conference of 1887 in London. The co-chairman, Lord Onslow, recalls that Deakin was the first native-born Australian to appear, and was impressed: "we could not help realising that we had before us a real, live man," he wrote, perhaps having been expecting a kangaroo. But the praise stood Deakin in good stead on his return to Melbourne.

His government was defeated in 1890, partly as a result of Deakin, as the responsible minister, sending in the troops to break a maritime strike. At the same time the land bubble burst, and Deakin, who had joined the speculative rush as a chairman or director of numerous somewhat shonky companies, found himself broke. By this time he was married to Pattie Browne, the daughter of a prominent (and formerly rich) spiritualist, and was forced to return to the law – this time, seriously. He made a success of it and paid off all his debts, in the process recovering the self-respect and confidence that had suffered a battering during the early years of the depression.

He was now ready for a new challenge. Throughout the '90s he had retained his seat in the Assembly as a backbencher, albeit an influential one; he described this period as "self-suppression in public life and continuous activity in private". But he also became involved in the federation movement, to which he had been first drawn by the 1887 conference; he realised that the colonies would have far more influence with Whitehall if they could speak with one voice. By 1895 he was acknowledged as the Victorian leader of the cause, and he played that role in the conventions of 1897 and 1898; in both he served on the constitutional committees.

He took the stance of a progressive and a democrat, albeit one committed to White Australia and the imperialist cause. His oratory was effective, but his political skills more important. Behind the scenes he became the federationists' chief enforcer and numbers man. He played a key role in the referendum campaign which followed, even converting his old employer, the *Age*. And he was an automatic choice as a member of the delegation to London which finally sold the constitution bill to Joseph Chamberlain and consequently the British Parliament.

The London trip had a totally unexpected consequence: Deakin accepted an offer from the *Morning Post* to become the paper's special correspondent, writing a weekly column and occasional specials on Australian politics. So first as Attorney-General, and later as Prime Minister, Deakin provided an anonymous account of the workings of his own government for the Tory readership of the *Post*. After 1904 he switched to the London *National Review*. It must be said that he did a good job: the accounts are comprehensive, witty and often highly critical, even of the Hon. Alfred Deakin. But it is hard not to see at least the possibility of a conflict of interest.

However, there is no actual evidence that this writing distracted him from his real work. As deputy to Barton, Deakin was the man chiefly responsible for ensuring the smooth running of the first, minority, government; in particular he had to keep the Labor Party, with whom the Protectionists were in an uneasy alliance against the opposition Free Traders, satisfied. This was not easy at the best of times, and the establishment of the arbitration commission, to which Deakin was a somewhat reluctant convert, was a constant point of friction. On the other hand he piloted the White Australia legislation through without difficulty. The High Court was more of a problem; he practically had to threaten resignation to gather the necessary votes to establish it.

Once the High Court was in place, Barton resigned to go to it, and Deakin, uncontested, became Prime Minister. He was swiftly thrown into the 1903 election campaign, and despite his best efforts the result was chaotic. His Protectionists returned twenty-six members, the Free Traders twenty-five and Labor twenty-three. Deakin, using a cricket analogy, referred to it as the period of "the three elevens" – he realised from the start that it could never provide stable government. He was swiftly proved correct; differences with Labor over the set-up of the arbitration commission finally proved intractable, and Deakin declared his innings and sent Labor's Chris Watson in to bat.

This solved nothing; after four months Deakin and the Free Traders' George Reid combined to defeat Labor, and Reid had his turn at the crease. What was seen as Deakin's defection to the common enemy caused great bitterness among the Labor stalwarts and exacerbated the ongoing feud between Deakin and the leading unions' advocate Billy Hughes. In one exchange during this period, provoked beyond endurance by Hughes's accusations of treachery, Deakin leapt to his feet and cried: "I deny it! I deny it! I deny it!" There was dead silence; Hughes stood mute, his hand cupped to his ear. The speaker asked if he had finished, and Hughes replied devastatingly: "Oh no, Mr Speaker. I was just waiting for the cock to crow."

Deakin, normally above the rough-and-tumble, on one occasion at least replied in kind. At the end of a speech defending his conduct in general terms, he suddenly changed tack: "And as for the gentleman who devoted so much time to attacking me and my works, I do not propose to reply to him except by saying to you that he presents as undignified a spectacle as does the ill-bred urchin whom one sees dragged from the tart shop, kicking and screaming as he goes."

In the event Reid's government lasted not much longer than Watson's had; Deakin changed sides again. He considered, with some justification, that he had taught both the other teams a lesson, and Labor at least concurred; the Protectionists were the lesser of two evils. Deakin returned to the chair, and to three years of relative stability. Even after the 1906 election, at which the Protectionists were reduced to just sixteen, compared to the Free Traders' twenty-seven and Labor's twenty-three, he remained in charge.

It was his most productive period: the arbitration commission issue was finally resolved, although the initial breakthrough had occured – improbably – during the Reid inter-regnum, and the doctrine of what Deakin called the "New Protectionism" was implemented; tariff protection was to be supplemented by a fair and equitable industrial relations system under which disputes would be resolved by conciliation and arbitration instead of tests of brute strength. After Henry Higgins's "Harvester" judgement of 1907, a basic wage was introduced, together with old-age pensions and other public welfare measures. Plans were drawn up for a transcontinental railway system and a start was made on an Australian navy.

But given the state of the parties in parliament, it was never going to last. In 1907 Chris Watson resigned as Labor leader, making way for Andrew Fisher, a much tougher opponent. Deakin had been attending an Imperial conference in London, where he had been unsuccessful in trying to persuade the British government to pay more attention to the Pacific; he returned in poor health and spirits. A year later Labor withdrew from its coalition with the Protectionists, and Fisher became Prime Minister with Deakin's reluctant backing; but the old ideologies were fading fast. The Free Traders had already rebranded themselves as the Anti-Socialists, and the Protectionists were split between hardliners and genuine Liberals. And with the rise of an increasingly militant Labor Party, new battlelines were being drawn.

Things came to a head in 1909. In what became known as the Fusion, Deakin led his moderates across the floor and into an alliance with the Anti-Socialists, now led by Joseph Cook. He became the first leader of a reformed Liberal Party. If Deakin's previous tergiversations had caused rumblings, now the protests went off the Richter scale. The outrage came not only from Labor, which promised a "war to the knife, with a stiletto finish"; some of Deakin's own former allies regarded his defection to the old enemy, in what appeared to be no more than a naked grab for power, as the ultimate betrayal.

One, Sir William Lyne, could not contain himself; as Deakin rose to address the house as Prime Minister once again, he screamed "Judas! Judas! Judas!" Billy Hughes grabbed the opportunity. "I heard from this side of the house some mention of Judas. I do not agree with that; it is not fair – to Judas, for whom there is this to be said, that he did not gag the man whom he betrayed, nor did he forbear to hang himself afterwards." Things only got worse; after one all-night session of vituperation the speaker of the house, Sir Frederick Holder, fell from his chair muttering "dreadful, dreadful" and was dead before morning.

Deakin's last, brief term in office did see some concrete achievements. National service was introduced, and the Commonwealth–state financial legislation was an attempt to put the relations between the central and state governments on some kind of secure footing. But the damage done to the conservative side by Deakin's many switches proved to be terminal, at least to the man himself. In the 1910 election, Labor won an absolute majority. Deakin hung around in opposition for a while, but the benches to the left of the speaker had never suited him. He departed in 1913 from what he once called "the nightmare – and daymare – of responsibility" to a quiet and introspective retirement.

His health, never robust, deteriorated quickly, but he did make a final public appearance at a 1917 pro-conscription rally being run by his old foe Billy Hughes at the MCG. A shared sense of patriotism and imperialism transcended any lingering personal animosity between the two. Deakin was too frail to address the crowd, but his message was published: "Fellow countrymen – I have lived and worked to help you keep Australia white and free. The supreme choice is given to you on December 20. On that day you can say the word that shall keep her name white and free forever. God in his wisdom has decreed that at this great crisis in our history my tongue must be silent owing to my failing powers. He alone knows how I yearn, my fellow Australians, to help you say that magic word ..." It is matter of record that they did not.

He died two years later, at the age of sixty-three, having declined all offers of honours, including a seat on the Privy Council, and even the appellation "Right Honourable". In his own words: "I act alone, live alone, and think alone." Alfred Deakin is certainly entitled to be considered one of our most significant prime ministers. The accolade bestowed on him by Robert Menzies, the "great builder", is appropriate; the legislation passed during his three separate governments laid much of the foundation for national policy, and if some of them have been superseded, some – notably the High Court, a system of industrial relations governed by law and a publicly run welfare system – have endured. And of course his important role in securing federation in the first place – "the birthday of a whole people", as he called it – cannot be overlooked.

But perhaps his outstanding contribution to Australian politics was that, after a lifetime of switching sides, he put in place the basic two-party structure we have today: Labor versus anti-Labor. The anti-Labor parties have had many names, but always the same policy: to keep Labor out of office. And it was Deakin's Fusion in 1909 that provided the prototype. He may have been a mystic, but he saw clearly the real and lasting political division in Australia. Sophocles, Burke, Mill and the rest must be proud of him.

JOHN CHRISTIAN **WATSON**

At first glance Chris Watson appears one of our least important prime ministers.

His four-month term of office was beaten for brevity only by the stop-gaps, and he passed no significant legislation. He left school at ten, was a poor orator and frequently suffered from ill health, both physical and emotional. As a final indignity he was expelled by his own party for deliberately opposing its policy on conscription.

And yet this undistinguished record masks one remarkable achievement: Watson led the first national Labor government, not only in Australia, but in the entire world. In spite of the above summary, he was an ideal candidate for the honour.

Born in 1867 in Valparaiso, Chile, he spent his childhood in New Zealand where he learned a trade as a printer's compositor. More significantly, he also became an active trade unionist. When he moved to Sydney in 1886, after a brief period working as a stablehand for the governor, Lord

Carrington (who once tipped him sixpence) found himself a job on the *Australian Star*.

He soon became father of the chapel (the senior union man on the paper) and a delegate to the NSW Trades and Labor Council, which was then examining the possibility of forming a political wing. This, of course, became the ALP. It stood candidates in the 1891 election and Watson was active in the campaign. Next year, at the age of twenty-four, Watson was also president of the TLC and chairman of the ALP national conference.

It was in this and subsequent conferences that Watson's political talents stood out. The delegates were a turbulent mixture of unionists, doctrinaire socialists, and members of the single-tax Henry George League. Watson was able not only to reconcile the competing interests, but weld them into a disciplined political organisation. He established the supremacy of the conference, whose decisions were to be binding on parliamentarians, and ensured that the unions retained a dominant position. And he pushed through the solidarity pledge, which bound individuals to support collective decisions. Although these rules have been watered down and made more flexible over time, they remain the essential framework of Australia's oldest continuously surviving political party.

Watson entered the NSW Parliament in 1894 and was once again revealed as a great conciliator: firm but fair, willing to listen to everyone but immovable when it came to principle. His integrity was shown when it came to the great issue of federation: he opposed the draft constitution as being insufficiently democratic, but that same commitment to democracy meant that it should be submitted to a referendum of the people and the people's verdict should be accepted. Thus he had no qualms about standing for election to the federal parliament in 1901, and emerged as the first member for the seat of Bland.

The Labor caucus of twenty-four met to elect a spokesman: they were not yet prepared to use the more authoritarian term leader. The obvious choice would have been Jim McGovern, who had been first-among-equals in the NSW parliamentary party, but he had failed in his bid for the federal house. Watson's only other serious rival, Billy Hughes, unaccountably missed the meeting. Watson got the nod, and it is fair to say that the party never regretted its choice.

In the NSW Assembly, Labor had held the balance of power between the Protectionists and Free Traders; now the same position applied in the House of Representatives, and it seemed to Watson that the same tactics should be used. These involved trading support for one of the major parties for concessions in policy, and while this had meant frequent and sometimes painful and acrimonious shifts of loyalty, it had proved reasonably effective.

As a staunch trade unionist, Watson's personal preference was for the Protectionists; moreover he had an admiration for Alfred Deakin which was to develop into a personal bond. Deakin returned the regard, praising Watson for his "soundness of judgement, clearness of argument and fairness to opponents ... his simple dignity, courage and resource". Thus initially Labor was in a loose partnership (though never formal coalition) with Edmund Barton and his successor, Deakin.

But a break came with the Commonwealth conciliation and arbitration commission. Labor policy was that it should cover state public servants; Deakin believed that would be too great an intrusion into the sovereignty of the elected government. Watson withdrew support, and Deakin, to the fury of the Free Traders who believed he would be forced to call an election, instead recommended to the Governor-General that Watson be offered a commission.

It was a truly revolutionary act: the conservatives could not believe it. Was the newly formed nation to be ruled by a rabble of labourers, miners and Irish nationalists, wild-eyed extremists dedicated to the overthrow of everything they valued? It was unthinkable. "This so-called government will exist entirely on sufferance," thundered the *Argus*, "and has no claim on an extended life." Privately Watson agreed; Labor was simply not ready for office.

In desperation Watson sought an alliance with the progressives in Deakin's party, but was knocked back. Charles Kingston would have been prepared to help out in a ministry, but was in very poor heath. Eventually Henry Higgins came to the rescue and agreed to serve as Watson's Attorney-General. "The poor fellows need encouragement," he confided to Alfred Deakin. He became a loyal member of the team and a confidant of Watson's, who, frustrated by his inability to get Labor objectives passed into legislation, admitted: "I despair of seeing any good come out of this government." Higgins remained loyal: "We came into office without cadging," he said, "and we shall go out without cringing."

And they did, with Deakin this time handing the baton to Reid. The Free Traders had now morphed into a party of vociferous anti-socialists, with Reid ranting about the "menace of the socialist tiger". But as Watson's brief term in office had demonstrated, a Labor government was nothing to worry about; they had been a bunch of pussycats, meticulous in every way. This was perhaps Watson's second great achievement: he had shown Labor could, under the strict rules he had helped to formulate, be trusted to sit – for at least a short spell – on the Treasury benches. It wasn't long – just six years in fact – before the electorate was prepared to trust them with an absolute majority.

In spite of his expressed wish to stand down, Watson was persuaded to stay on as leader in opposition, and was instrumental in bringing down Reid and re-installing Deakin for his second term. He handed over to Andrew Fisher in 1907 and left parliament altogether in 1910. But he remained active in the Labor movement, while building up business interests and pursuing long-missed leisure time; he had been a keen sportsman in his youth and still liked a bet and a beer. In later years he was involved in the soldier settlement scheme, was president of the NRMA for twenty years and became the first chairman of Ampol and a trustee of the Sydney Cricket Ground. His mature years were respectable and comfortable.

But he had broken with the ALP; in 1916 he actively campaigned for conscription, and was automatically expelled under the solidarity rules he had helped to create. However, the party's affection and respect for his long service ensured that he was never anathematised as his old colleague Billy Hughes was. When he died in 1941 John Curtin, recently installed as Labor's fifth Prime Minister, himself provided a eulogy. Forgiven for being a rat, Watson remained an icon – at least in the party he helped to found.

GEORGE HOUSTOUN **REID**

HISTORY HAS TREATED George Houstoun Reid badly – largely because history is written by the winners. In this case the winner was Alfred Deakin who loathed our fourth Prime Minister, undermined his career, crippled his brief time in office and eventually hounded him out of politics altogether.

Deakin's assessment of Reid as "inordinately vain and resolutely selfish" – also cunning, vituperative and shallow – has been widely quoted, but it was Deakin's savage description of his enemy that was adopted by the caricaturists and has become the basis of much that has been written about him since: "his immense, unwieldy, jelly-like stomach, always threatening to break his waistband, his little legs apparently bowed under its weight to the verge of their endurance, his thick neck rising behind his ears to his many-folded chin. His protuberant blue eyes were expressionless until roused or half-hidden in cunning [and] a blond complexion and an infantile breadth of baldness gave him an air of insolent juvenility." Affable Alfred certainly had a way with words.

Another long time foe, Sir Henry Parkes, dismissed Reid as "a babbling idiot"; which may have had something to do with the fact that Reid twice outpolled him in the multi-member electorate of East Sydney (he once even beat Edmund Barton in the same seat). It is certainly true that Reid was a rambunctious, even vulgar, politician; it was said that people attended his campaign meetings purely for their entertainment value. But his larger-than-life appearance and demeanour concealed a mind which was not only politically astute, but one of the most progressive of his time. Of all our early politicians, Reid is the one most deserving of the term "liberal".

He was born in Scotland in 1845, and the family migrated to Melbourne in 1852. After school at Scotch College, Reid moved to Sydney and entered the colonial public service. Although he described himself as a duffer, he rose swiftly through the Treasury and simultaneously studied law; in 1878 he became secretary to the Crown Law Office and in 1880 won a seat in the Legislative Assembly.

From the start he was a champion of free trade, but he believed that the same liberal principles should extend to other areas. He favoured universal suffrage and drastic tax reform, including the use of a land tax and a direct income tax to replace customs tariffs and, almost uniquely for the time, he opposed harsh laws against the Chinese. Inevitably he fell out with the Premier and leader of the Free Trade Party, Sir Henry Parkes, and generally preferred to sit with the opposition.

When Alexander Stuart became Premier in 1882 he offered Reid the Treasury, but Reid preferred Public Instruction – what would now be called Education. He sorted out the problems of the newly formed public primary schools, established the public high school system, and laid the foundations for technical education and evening courses at Sydney University. But when Parkes returned as Premier in 1891 Reid refused to serve under him; he now saw himself as the real leader of the free trade movement. Parkes eventually retired and at the 1894 election Reid's Free Traders – now also known as the Liberal Party – won just short of a majority in their own right. With the support of Labor Reid was Premier and Treasurer for five years, during which he was able to institute most of the economic reforms he considered necessary to revive his state and make it competitive with Victoria. Labor withdrew its support in 1899 and Reid was able to turn his attention full time to the cause of federation, which he had previously regarded as a distraction from his principal task.

He did, however, attend the 1897 Imperial conference in London, where he found himself seated between the Prince of Wales and the Archbishop of Canterbury at the concluding banquet. Aware of his tendency to nod off after a good meal, Reid asked the startled prelate to make sure he stayed awake through the speeches; he was never one for protocol.

Back in Australia, he agreed with Parkes about the need for federation but was not prepared to compromise his principles to achieve it; compelling free trade New South Wales to federate with the other protectionist colonies would, he said, be like forcing a teetotaller to share a house with five drunkards. His ambivalence led to the celebrated incident when he returned from the 1898 convention and addressed a meeting at Sydney Town Hall. As Jack Lang recounted, "he started off by saying that he proposed to address himself to the problem as if he was a judge summing up for the benefit of a jury. Then he carefully enunciated the arguments in favour of federation. Then he switched sides and just as carefully set out the case in opposition. In all he spoke for two hours and when he had concluded his audience was completely in the dark as to whether he was for or against the proposition. From that time he became known as Yes-No Reid."

He was, however, easily elected to the Commonwealth parliament of 1901 where he became leader of the official opposition. He knew Barton from their time together in the Legislative Assembly, and got on well with him; while Barton remained Prime Minister he was cordial and co-operative. But things changed in 1903 when Deakin took the chair.

The relationship became antagonistic; but even in those early days Reid foresaw that the real political conflict would be between the rising Labor Party and the supporters of private enterprise. During Chris Watson's brief time in power, Reid noted that Deakin was now realising the truth about his former Labor allies: "he found that the voters who returned them were pawns, that the members who were returned were dummies and that the ministers of that party were figureheads. He also discovered that their methods of organisation outside and their methods inside were such as were subversive of the true principles of parliamentary government. I cordially agreed with him in that view."

When Watson's government fell and Reid was commissioned, he suggested an anti-socialist coalition with the Protectionists, but Deakin refused and his party effectively split, giving Reid a majority of just two in the House of

Representatives and a minority in the Senate. His government lasted less than a year and was unmemorable except for one achievement; it finally passed the Conciliation and Arbitration Act, the issue which had bedevilled the parliament since its inauguration and brought down two prime ministers. Reid, the great anti-socialist, was the one who legislated Labor's most basic demand for the law to apply to state public servants.

In 1905 Deakin returned to office with Labor's support; Reid stayed on as an anti-socialist crusader but finally resigned in 1908. With his old enemy out of the way, Deakin and the new party leader Joseph Cook merged their parties in the anti-Labor Fusion, thus fulfilling Reid's prophecy and hope. In 1910 he accepted appointment as high commissioner to London, a job then as now eminently well suited to his ebullient lifestyle. When compelled to make way for Andrew Fisher in 1916, he was offered, and accepted, a seat in the UK House of Commons, which he occupied until his death in 1918.

He was, in his own way, a consummate politician – even something of a statesman, frequently putting what he saw as the national interest ahead of his own. He died festooned with Imperial honours, but what people recall is the caricature, the clown who, when heckled at a meeting by a man who pointed at his ample belly and asked: "What are you going to call it, George?" had the wit to reply: "If it's a boy I'll call it after myself. If it's a girl, I'll call it Victoria. But if, as I strongly suspect, it's nothing but piss and wind, I'll name it after you."

And he may have been capable of even better: a classic political anecdote is that of the politician, who, when heckled by a woman who hissed "you are a dreadful man – if you were my husband I'd put poison in your tea," responded: "And, madam, if you were my wife, I'd drink it." This politician is usually identified as the young Winston Churchill, but there is a school of thought which gives the credit to George Houstoun Reid. For that alone he deserves an honoured place in history.

ANDREW FISHER

ANDREW FISHER'S PLACE in history is secure: he led the Labor Party for eight years and had three separate terms as Prime Minister, a feat equalled only by Alfred Deakin.

More significantly, for two of those terms his party held an absolute majority, the first to do so. He established the Labor Party as a central force in Australian politics and left behind an impressive record of legislation. But perhaps the most surprising aspect of his brilliant career was that he achieved all this while spending less than half his life in Australia. The native son he was not.

Fisher was born in 1862 in Ayrshire, Scotland, to a coal-mining family and followed his father into the pits at an early age – by some accounts as young as ten, although the legal minimum age for children to work in the mines was twelve. It was a grim start to his working life, and what little leisure time he had was not exactly riotous either. The Fishers belonged to a particularly dour and disciplined section of the Presbyterian Church known locally as the "Wee Free";

they were the kind of Calvinists of whom it used to be said that they disapproved of sex because it might lead to dancing.

So Fisher was perforce of a serious nature, and his passions were channelled into a militant embrace of the infant trades union movement. By the time he was seventeen he was secretary of his local branch; the union's general secretary was the great labour hero Keir Hardie, who became something of a mentor to the young man, persuading him to undertake evening classes and introducing him to art and literature.

Emboldened, Fisher led a strike by his branch in 1881, but it turned into a complete disaster: the strike was broken after ten weeks, the union wiped out and Fisher himself was blacklisted. For the next three years he found sporadic work only, and helped to reform the union in 1884, but his prospects in Ayrshire were not hopeful. Many other Scots were also despairing of ever finding prosperity at home; it was a time of migration to the various new worlds. Fisher, together with his younger brother James, joined the diaspora and in 1885 disembarked in Brisbane.

The brothers found work in the Burrum coalfields, but after being rejected for promotion Andrew Fisher moved to Gympie and quickly joined the local miners' union. He became secretary in 1890 and president the following year, when the shearers' strike led to the formation of the Labor Party. Fisher became the first president of the Gympie branch and was elected to the Queensland Legislative Assembly in 1893.

He had an impressive physical presence, suiting his militant stance, but his manner was described by contemporaries as always quiet and conciliatory. It was certainly appropriate to those early days, when Labor was a minority party which could only hope to influence policy by co-operating with one of the major parties. Although he was an unapologetic socialist, Fisher realised that his time had not yet come, so he concentrated on attempting to modify capitalism, not destroying it. He supported the liberal ideas of industrial arbitration, universal education, progressive taxation, a state bank and workers' protection, but failed to achieve change.

He lost his seat in the 1896 election and returned to Gympie, where he founded a newspaper the *Gympie Truth* to counter the anti-Labor *Gympie Times*. Presumably it worked; he was re-elected in 1899, and in December became a minister in the government of Anderson Dawson, the first Labor administration of any kind anywhere in the world. It lasted just six days, but Fisher's disappointment was brief. He now had his sights set firmly on the federal sphere, and in 1901 was elected as the first member for Wide Bay.

He was quickly accepted as a member of the leadership group, along with Chris Watson and Billy Hughes, and was given the Ministry for Trade and Customs in Watson's short-lived government. But he clashed with Watson over a key political question at the 1905 ALP conference. Watson was a coalitionist; he wanted Labor to form alliances where compatible aims could be found. Fisher insisted that the party must remain independent; alliances would compromise not only its integrity but its viability as a coherent political force.

He won, and Watson offered his resignation. He was persuaded to stay on as leader, but Fisher became his deputy, to the frustration of Hughes. This frustration was compounded in 1907 when Watson retired for good and Fisher beat Hughes for the succession, reportedly by just one vote. Their rivalry was the backdrop for the entire eight years of Fisher's leadership but, to the credit of both, did not hinder the party's political progress.

While Fisher was never as close to Deakin as Watson had been, the two men got on reasonably well. But the Labor caucus, having tasted power once, was impatient for more. It withdrew support for Deakin at the end of 1908 and his government fell; Fisher became Prime Minister. His was a minority government: it still depended for its existence on the support of what was left of the Protectionists. But from the start Fisher refused to compromise. He introduced Labor legislation in the full knowledge that it would be rejected and foreshadowed referendums designed to amend the constitution and greatly expand the powers of the Commonwealth.

It was too much for Deakin, who led his followers into the Fusion with the Anti-Socialists under their new leader Joseph Cook. For Fisher the split with Deakin was final and absolute: "What can you do with a man like that?" he demanded of his caucus. Labor was now irrevocably on its own. Deakin once again took over as Prime Minister, but a general election was due in 1910 and the next nine months were spent by the respective parties manoeuvring for the most favourable issue on which to fight it. Fisher easily won the tactical battle and went to the 1910 double dissolution with vigour and confidence; he won 43 of the 75 seats in the House of Representatives, and 23 of the 36 seats in the Senate. Labor ruled, and embarked on a swift and widespread program of change.

The next three years saw the formation of a national defence force; the inauguration of the Commonwealth Bank; the start of the Port Augusta to Kalgoorlie railway, which Western Australia had demanded as the price of joining federation; and the selection of Canberra as the national capital. National service was proclaimed and a land tax implemented. Fisher legislated for old-age pensions, workers compensation and maternity allowances, which had all been in Deakin's platform but had never gone through parliament. Importantly, he gave legal preference to union members in Commonwealth employment. He also had time for a spot of overseas travel, to South Africa for the inauguration of the Union and to London for the coronation of George V. On the latter trip he made a triumphal return to Ayrshire and received a hero's welcome.

The pace was frantic; perhaps too frantic for the electorate, which took a breather in 1913 by voting Labor out by 1 seat. But Labor retained control of the Senate, making a double-dissolution election necessary to break the deadlock. After just one year Cook bowed to the inevitable and went back to the people, who unceremoniously ejected him and restored Fisher.

In the meantime the Great War had broken out in Europe. Fisher, like Hughes, had opposed Australia sending troops to fight for Britain in the Boer War, but he now assumed the stance of a patriotic imperialist: "we stand beside our own to help and defend her to the last man and the last shilling," he promised an election meeting, and repeated the pledge as Prime Minister. As a war leader he was able to capitalise on the birth of the Gallipoli legend; by the end of 1915 he was, it appeared, at the height of his political powers, destined for a long and fruitful term as Prime Minister. And then, in October, he suddenly resigned from both the leadership and parliament and took up the job of Agent-General, the federal government's representative in London.

The common belief is that Hughes had finally amassed the numbers in caucus, and made Fisher an offer he could not refuse. But this seems too glib. Hughes had never had the numbers before; he had mounted a challenge after the electoral defeat of 1913 and Fisher had seen him off easily. It was hardly likely that he had made up so much ground during the time of Fisher's triumph. It is true that some sections of caucus were unhappy at the wartime restrictions the government had felt compelled to impose, but Hughes was certainly not going to change that.

Another story goes that Fisher himself was determined to force a showdown and offered Hughes the Agent-General job; when Hughes refused, Fisher replied: "Very well, I'll take it myself." This has the ring of urban myth, but it is quite possible that Fisher was looking for an excuse to retire. His health, never good, deteriorated drastically from the start of 1914 and at the beginning of 1915 he had actually taken what amounted to a rest cure in New Zealand. There is little doubt that this time he intended the move to be permanent; before leaving he dedicated Oakleigh Hall, the Melbourne mansion he had bought for his family, as a convalescent home for returned soldiers. He made just one brief return visit to Australia before his death in 1928.

London indeed proved a retirement. As Prime Minister Hughes took personal control of wartime negotiations between Australia and Whitehall, so Fisher's role as

Agent-General became largely ceremonial. He served on the Dardanelles Commission and visited Australian troops in France but that was about it; he was out of politics. He once again infuriated Hughes by refusing to support the pro-conscription campaign, relying on the principle of public service neutrality. Apart from a desultory and failed attempt to secure one of the Scottish seats in the House of Commons he dropped out of sight until succumbing to his now chronic ill health.

Fisher was not a shining star in the political sky; the historian John La Nauze dismissed him as "a man of integrity whose place in his party and public reputation depended on a rock-like lack of brilliance". But this is to underrate him. Apart from his obviously successful career, Fisher was something of a trailblazer. If Watson had shown that Labor politicians did not have horns and tails, it was Fisher who demonstrated that they could be trusted with the reins of government.

He was, despite his upbringing, something of a progressive. In the 1908 conference he argued for the place of women in politics: "I trust that not another federal election will take place without there being a woman endorsed as a Labor candidate for the Senate." It was not until 1943 that Dorothy Tangney was elected to the upper house.

Fisher never strayed far from first principles. At the same conference he asserted that due to the entry of Labor into politics, socialism had moved from "being tabooed and sneered at and had been brought to a first place in public discussion ... we are all socialists now and the only qualification you hear from anybody is probably that he is not an extreme socialist. I do not think the idea of the originators have altered one jot." Inflexible, and perhaps not much of a prediction of how the party was to develop. But it was precisely that conviction and assurance that made Andrew Fisher the right man to bring Labor into the political mainstream.

He is rightly revered by his party as a true believer and great achiever. As another historian, Clem Lloyd, put it: "No-one has led the party better. Probably only Curtin has led it as well." Illustrious company indeed.

JOSEPH **COOK**

IF THERE WAS ever a contest to decide who was Australia's least memorable Prime Minister, Joseph Cook (or Cooke – even his name was changeable) would be a strong contender.

Others have had briefer stints at the top: Frank Forde served for just eight days, and is remembered for precisely that reason. Cook lasted fifteen months, but they were fifteen months of spectacular non-achievement.

He was a drab and colourless figure; unlike his mentor, George Reid, he left no record of wit or flamboyance. Cook's term in office is recalled, if it is recalled at all, only as a hiccup in the government of Andrew Fisher.

But Cook deserves more, if not necessarily better, from history. His political career was a long and steady progress from pit boy at the mines to the Privy Council as a knight of the realm. And it included at least one act for which he will not be forgotten nor forgiven: Joseph Cook was the first of the Labor rats.

He was born in 1860 in the Staffordshire mining town of

Silverdale and was sent to the collieries as a pit boy at the age of nine. He was thirteen when his father was killed in a mining accident, and he became a fully fledged miner, moonlighting as a Methodist lay preacher.

The local Methodists had strong links with the trades union movement and the young man became active in the cause, taking part in two major strikes. Defeated in both and now married, his thoughts turned to emigration; a brother-in-law at Lithgow wrote glowingly of the prospects for miners in Australia. In 1885 he took the plunge, leaving his young family to join him when he became established.

He quickly did so, supplementing his income from the mines by learning shorthand and accounting and working part-time as an auditor. He became general secretary of the union and a founding member of the Labor Party branch; a seat in the NSW Legislative Assembly was the next logical step, and he was elected in 1891 on a radical platform which included the eight-hour work day and votes for women.

Cook was chosen as leader of the parliamentary Labor Party in 1893, but was never comfortable with the discipline the party sought to impose. When the 1894 conference passed a resolution binding all members of the caucus to follow majority decisions, he refused to sign the solidarity pledge and resigned forthwith. Several other members did likewise, but Cook was the only one to accept a ministry from Labor's sworn enemy, the Free Trade Premier, George Reid. This was the unpardonable treachery which earned him a place on Labor's permanent hate list.

Cook had a productive time under Reid as Postmaster-General and Secretary for Mines and became a disciple of his charismatic leader; he shared Reid's "yes-no" ambivalence towards federation, but quickly followed him into the first federal parliament. To his surprise and annoyance he was not given a post in Reid's short-lived government, but when it fell in 1905 he was elected as deputy leader and heir apparent.

He was now firmly established on an upwardly mobile path: in parliament he spoke disparagingly of "the working classes and their economic theories", and he bought a house in Baulkham Hills, the most exclusive part of his Parramatta electorate. The Labor movement was not only discarded; it had become the irrevocable foe.

Cook succeeded Reid as leader of the Free Trade (now Anti-Socialist) Party in 1908, and quickly entered a partnership with Alfred Deakin's Protectionists to defeat the minority Labor government. This became the Fusion, the basis of the permanent conservative anti-Labor alliance; and while it was Reid's idea, it was his protégé who actually implemented it.

Cook enjoyed a brief period in government as Deakin's deputy and Minister for Defence. In the latter capacity he set up a system of compulsory military training and hosted a visit by Lord Kitchener. But Labor easily won the 1910 poll with an absolute majority, cementing Cook's unenviable record: he had been in parliament for a decade without ever having been on the side that won an election.

He finally broke his duck in 1913: Deakin had retired and Cook became Prime Minister. But it was a Pyrrhic victory. In the House of Representatives he had a shaky majority of one, and Labor controlled the Senate. There was no prospect of implementing a conservative legislative program, so instead Cook spent his time setting up the conditions for a double-dissolution election which he hoped would give him control of both houses. It didn't; in 1914 Andrew Fisher's Labor government was overwhelmingly returned.

Cook's career appeared to be effectively over, but the great Labor split over conscription for World War I gave him another opportunity. He joined Billy Hughes's minority to form the Nationalists – a party that had the distinction of being born from the marriage of two Labor rats.

Cook disliked and distrusted Hughes, who had been his most scathing critic after his 1894 defection, but was content to serve as his deputy. The pair went to London in 1918 and sat in the Imperial War Cabinet, attending the Imperial War Conference. Cook returned to Silverdale and hometown acclaim, but perhaps the most satisfying accolade came from British diplomat Sir Harold Nicolson, who was mightily impressed by Cook's performance as a delegate on the committee on Czechoslovakia, which was part of the post-war peace conference. Nicolson wrote approvingly: "Old Cook is all right. He has sense. The French the other day started an endless argument about the Delbruck nationalist laws. When the whole thing had been translated into English, old Cook was asked to record his views. 'Damn Delbruck' was what he said."

Back in Australia Cook became Treasurer under Hughes, a role in which he was ineffective in controlling growing unemployment. He resigned in 1921 and returned to London as high commissioner, where he reportedly threw himself into the city's social life; his strict Methodism was, like his youthful radicalism, now well behind him. He came back to Sydney in 1927 and built a block of flats in Bellevue Hill, where he lived until his death in 1947.

At least one contemporary had a kind word for him. Billy Hughes praised his political skills and declared that his friend Joe had been both loyal and loveable. The ALP faithful laughed scornfully. Just what would Billy Hughes, the archetypal rat, know about either quality?

WILLIAM MORRIS **HUGHES**

Billy Hughes said he was born in Wales; he wasn't, he was born in Pimlico, a London suburb. He said the year was 1864; it wasn't, it was 1862. He said his interest in the classics had been awakened when the poet Matthew Arnold presented him with a copy of the works of Shakespeare. Well, perhaps. With Hughes it was often hard to tell where truth ended and fantasy began.

But what is certain is that despite suffering from congenital deafness and chronic dyspepsia he was a member of Australian parliaments continuously for fifty-eight years, fifty-one of them in the federal House of Representatives. He was in at the birth of six political parties, led five of them, served as a minister in four of them and ratted on three. It is a political record unlikely to be beaten.

William Morris Hughes was the son of a carpenter and a farmer's daughter. He had a rudimentary education but at the age of twelve became a pupil-teacher at St Stephen's School at Westminster; obviously his talent for selling himself developed at an early age. He emigrated for reasons unknown in 1884 and spent a couple of years roughing it through the outback, a period he later romanticised in terms worthy of Banjo Paterson. He finally settled in Sydney and after a period of odd-jobbery married his landlady's daughter and opened a shop in Balmain. Even in his youth he was said to have the appearance of a wizened gnome, which in later life became a gift to the cartoonists. But his energy and liveliness belied this look of premature senility.

It was a fortunate coincidence of time and place: Hughes's shop became a meeting place for young reformers and radicals such as William Holman and George Beeby. Hughes joined first the Single Tax League of Henry George, and then the Socialist League. He became a fiery street-corner orator and spent eight months out west as an organiser for the Amalgamated Shearers' Union, before returning to gain preselection for the Labor Party in 1894. Hughes records that his preselection meeting ended in a riot and he was forced to run for his life; certainly, they were lively times. When he won the seat of Lang, he was paraded through the streets in a dog-cart, wearing a suit bought by his supporters.

In the NSW Legislative Assembly he soon made his mark; at first Labor had supported George Reid's Free Traders, but in 1899 Hughes was influential in persuading the party to switch to William Lyne. He had brought down his first government.

His power base was the trades union movement. The failure of the 1890 maritime strike had crushed the wharfies. Hughes restored them as a major industrial force, and also became secretary of the Trolley, Draymen and Carters'

Union. He persuaded the militant union leaders that the strike weapon should only be used as a last resort and achieved significant gains through bargaining and arbitration. By the time he went into federal parliament in 1901 he was known and respected as the unions' leading advocate, an industrial Mr Fixit.

In his seat of West Sydney he became part of the Labor leadership group, where he specialised in industrial relations and defence. He argued passionately for a system of national service, which was eventually introduced in 1909. In Chris Watson's fleeting government he served as Minister for External Affairs and headed a royal commission into the pay and conditions of merchant seamen.

This led Alfred Deakin to send him to London for a conference on the subject. He returned via the United States and wrote a number of articles about his experiences; as a result the conservative *Daily Telegraph* offered him a weekly column to be called "The Case for Labor". Hughes snapped it up and it quickly became both popular and influential, doing much to improve the image of the ALP among cautious middle-class voters. In the same year, 1907, Hughes became Andrew Fisher's deputy and served as Attorney-General in the short-lived government of 1908.

When this government ended with the conservative Fusion, Deakin became Hughes's bitter enemy and the target of some of his most memorable invective. In one of the milder outbursts he thundered: "What a career his has been! In his hands, at various times, have rested the banners of every party in the country. He has proclaimed them all, he has held them all and he has betrayed them all ... last night the honourable member abandoned the finer resources of political assassination and resorted to the bludgeon of the cannibal." It was a speech Hughes's opponents often recalled when considering his own subsequent career.

Hughes remained Attorney-General in Fisher's subsequent governments and finally succeeded to the leadership he believed was rightfully his in 1915. He had already taken a leading role in the war effort, introducing legislation to control the supply of basic raw materials including food, wool and metals. Now he became the public face of patriotism, and as such made a trip to London in 1916 where he received a riotous reception. He took part in a speaking tour which was so successful that the popular press even speculated that he might replace the war-weary Prime Minister Henry Asquith as the Empire's war leader – a suggestion so improbable that neither he nor Asquith found it necessary to comment.

A David Low cartoon showed Hughes dancing on the British cabinet table with a nervous Asquith imploring David Lloyd George: "David, talk to him in Welsh and pacify him!" But in spite of his popularity, Hughes was unable to gain political support for his plans to attack German interests in the Pacific. He ended his trip with a visit to the Australian troops on the front-line in France, a move which enhanced his reputation both at home and abroad.

Back in Australia enthusiasm for the war was on the wane. Hughes saw that his plans for conscription had little chance of passing through parliament, so he went straight to the people with a referendum. Resistance came from Irish Australians bitter about the English treatment of the 1916 Easter Rising, but also from the trades unions, worried that conscripted workers would be replaced with cheap labour. In the end the referendum was narrowly lost, and Hughes's ascendancy with it.

A special caucus meeting was called to deal with the result: militants wanted Hughes expelled for having breached party policy by his advocacy of conscription. Hughes brought matters to a head by walking out: "Let all who support me follow me!" he cried, and twenty-four of the sixty-five Labor members did so, although one later went back. Hughes's version of events was typically idiosyncratic: "I did not leave the party. The party left me." When John Curtin later accused him of trying to smash the Labor Party, Hughes replied: "I couldn't do that. No one can smash the Labor Party." Perhaps, but the first great split left Labor in opposition for thirteen years.

It also left Hughes as Prime Minister; he formed his rump of followers into the National Labor Party and continued to govern with the support of the Liberal opposition. At the start of 1917 the alliance was formalised: the two parties merged as the Nationalists. Although Hughes's supporters were in the minority, Hughes remained the leader: the Liberals' Joseph Cook realised that he could not compete.

Hughes led his new party to a landslide win in the 1917 election on a pro-war platform. Emboldened, he proposed a new referendum on conscription, promising – or rather threatening – to resign if it was again defeated. But the opposition was both more organised and more determined than before. The Catholic archbishop of Melbourne, Daniel Mannix, joined T.J. Ryan, the Queensland Labor Premier, in a ferocious campaign. When Hughes addressed a meeting in Warwick, in Ryan's home state, a dissenter threw an egg at him, knocking his hat off; Hughes ordered a local police sergeant to arrest the offender, and when the sergeant refused, returned to Melbourne and founded the Commonwealth police force for his protection.

In the end, the referendum was decisively lost, and Hughes offered his resignation. But he had already taken the precaution of nobbling any possible rivals, so he was recommissioned as Prime Minister on the same day. His only real threat came from the ageing Sir John Forrest: Hughes went to the extraordinary length of demanding that London confer a peerage on his rival so that he could be sent off to the House of Lords. As it happened the move was unnecessary; Lord Forrest of Bunbury died of cancer on the voyage to England.

Hughes was now, it seemed, untouchable. In 1918 he returned to London to sit in the Imperial War Cabinet; when peace was declared he stayed on, and insisted that he be made an independent delegate to the Versailles conference. To the irritation of some of the major players, Hughes took an active role.

One of those who suffered was the American president, Woodrow Wilson, who sat with Hughes on a committee formed to discuss the mandated control of the former German colonies. Hughes demanded details of the proposals. Wilson replied that they were not yet final. Hughes said in that event Australia would not agree to proceed until they were. Wilson asked incredulously if this was an ultimatum. Hughes replied that it was.

Wilson, drawing on his full pomposity, addressed himself to Hughes: "Mr Prime Minister of Australia, do I understand your attitude aright? If I do, it is this, that the opinion of the whole civilised world is to be set at nought.

This conference, fraught with such infinite consequences to mankind for good or evil, is to break up with results which may well be disastrous to the future happiness of eighteen hundred millions of the human race, in order to satisfy the whim of five million people in the remote southern continent whom you claim to represent." In one version of the story Hughes fiddled with his hearing aid and asked the president to repeat his speech. But in all of them, he eventually replied approvingly: "Very well put, Mr President, you have guessed it. That's just about the size of it." Chided again about the smallness of the Australian population, he said bluntly: "I represent sixty thousand dead."

In the event Australia ended up with a 599-year mandate over Papua New Guinea and Hughes was able to block a Japanese call for a clause on racial equality to be included in the covenant of the League of Nations. On his return to London Australian troops clapped a slouch hat on his head and chaired him through the streets, cheering their Little Digger. He returned home on a troopship to a similar triumph. It was probably his finest hour.

But a jaded civilian population was not so supportive. As well as shortages and a host of regulations, the war years had brought them income tax, death duties and an entertainment tax. Hughes's attempt to spring a khaki election in 1919 backfired: the Nationalists were reduced to minority status. A new group, the Country Party, had emerged and Hughes had to rely on independents to give him the numbers.

Nonetheless, his last term as Prime Minister was his most productive. He set up the independent Tariff Board (the precursor of the Productivity Commission) and the Institute of Science and Industry, which became the CSIRO.

He formed a Department of Civil Aviation and the Commonwealth Oil Refineries. A fleet of sixteen merchant ships purchased on a previous visit to England became the foundation of the Commonwealth Shipping Line, and a return visit led to the establishment of Amalgamated Wireless, which made Australia the only member of the Commonwealth besides Britain itself to have an independent overseas radio service. Hughes also persuaded Britain, the United States, France and Japan to sign a treaty of co-operation in the Pacific. This fulfilled his life-long ambition to put a limit on Japanese influence.

It was a time of high achievement, but it came to an end with the 1922 elections, which saw the Nationalists' numbers further eroded by an expanding Country Party and a re-formed Liberal Party. And even within the Nationalists there were complaints of Hughes's dictatorial and manipulative style of government. The revelation that his admirers had made him a secret gift of £25,000 – a small fortune – did not help. The Country Party, under its forceful leader Earle Page, refused point-blank to co-operate with Hughes and in 1923 he was forced to relinquish the leadership to his Treasurer, Stanley Bruce.

He retired to the backbench and cultivated his public persona as a colourful, sometimes even outrageous, super-patriot, never missing an Anzac Day parade. But he continued to plot to regain power, and in 1929 the opportunity came. Bruce moved to gut the Commonwealth Arbitration Commission and Hughes managed to hive off enough Nationalists to defeat his motion. Hughes was noted for his "sphinx-like smile" at the outcome. Bruce accepted the loss as a vote of no confidence and lost both the subsequent election and his own seat. It was the effective end of the Nationalists; Hughes left the party and stood as an independent.

Throughout the Labor government of James Scullin he worked to form a new centre party to be known as the Australian Party, but support was slow and sporadic. When Joseph Lyons left the Labor Party and joined the conservatives as leader of what became the United Australia Party, Hughes was happy to join his fellow rat. In 1934 Lyons gave him the junior Health Ministry and later promoted him to External Affairs, but he was forced to resign after publishing a book critical of the League of Nations' failure to act against Mussolini's invasion of Abyssinia.

Government policy was to do nothing to offend the emerging European dictators, but Hughes, as always, was more forthright. When a reporter asked for his views on Adolf Hitler he replied: "I'm only Minister for External Affairs – I'm not allowed to say anything, so therefore I cannot comment. I will, of course, say that if you paved the way from here to Broken Hill with bibles and that man Hitler swore an oath on every one of them, I wouldn't believe a goddam bloody word he said."

When Lyons died in 1939 Hughes made a bid for the party leadership but lost narrowly to Robert Menzies. He did, however, become Menzies's deputy, and when Menzies was forced to resign in 1941, took over to become deputy Prime Minister under Arthur Fadden. He served on John Curtin's advisory war council as leader of the United Australia Party until Menzies took over in 1943, and continued to do so even after the UAP voted formally to withdraw from it in 1944; it was his last act of defiance, and his last taste of power.

In 1945 Menzies invited him to join the new Liberal Party but refused him a ministry. Hughes sat, always hopeful, on the backbench until his death in 1952. His last public act was to be the face of Australia in the celebration of the fiftieth anniversary of federation: Jubilee Hughes.

There is a famous story which sums up both the man and his career. At a tribute dinner for the great survivor, it was noted that he had, in his time, been a member of every political party in Australian history bar the Country Party – why the exception? In one version the occasion is 1944 and the interlocutor John Curtin; in another the year is 1951 and the interlocutor Arthur Fadden. But in all versions Hughes's reply is the same: "I had to draw the line somewhere."

Irreverent, witty and charming. Also, of course, devious, unreliable, authoritarian, ill-tempered, untrustworthy and disloyal. Unquestionably, one of the great characters not only of Australian politics, but of Australian history.

STANLEY MELBOURNE **BRUCE**

THE MAN WHO succeeded Billy Hughes could not have been more different from his rag-tag, larrikin predecessor.

The picture that most often emerges of Stanley Melbourne Bruce is that of the leading man in a silent movie: tall, handsome and elegant in plus-fours and spats, leaning against a late-model sports car with a rich and glamorous wife on his arm, the ultimate gentleman aristocrat, more English than the English.

It is the image of a man destined for success, even for greatness. And yet where Australian politics is concerned, Bruce has become a byword for failure: the reluctant Prime Minister who achieved little in office, left his country's economy in ruins and was so out of touch that he even lost his seat in the election which swept him from power, a humiliation duplicated only by John Howard some sixty-eight years later. A bumpy ride indeed.

It all started promisingly enough. Bruce was born in 1883, the son of a wealthy importer who gave him his middle name to honour the city which brought him wealth and power; to have immortalised the suburb, Toorak, would have been a bit much. The boy was sent to the prestigious Melbourne Grammar School, where he became school captain and led the football, cricket and rowing teams, thence to Cambridge to study law and pick up a rowing blue. He then moved to the capital to head the family firm's London office at a lavish salary of £5000 a year.

He returned briefly to Australia in 1913 to wed the heiress Ethel Dunlop Anderson, but on the outbreak of war went back to England to enlist in the Inns of Court regiment. He was wounded at Gallipoli and again in France, won a Military Cross and a Croix de Guerre, and was repatriated from the army with the rank of captain in 1916. At this stage it seemed likely he would live out his career as a successful businessman based in London, but in 1917 a brother who had been looking after the firm's Melbourne office died unexpectedly and Bruce was recalled to take temporary charge.

He used the visit to enter the campaign for conscription, and was immediately recognised as a likely candidate for the newly formed Nationalist Party: his looks, wealth and record in business and the military made him irresistibly electable. After some hesitation he agreed to stand for the seat of Flinders, which he won easily. But his business interests always came first, and he spent more time in London than in the Spring Street parliament.

Once again fate intervened; he was on a golfing holiday in Le Touquet in 1921 when an urgent request came from Prime Minister Billy Hughes for him to represent Australia as a delegate to the League of Nations meeting in Geneva.

He agreed, and on his return Hughes, desperate for ministers who would impress the big end of town, offered him the Ministry of Trade and Customs. Bruce, sensing an opportunity, declined: for the active head of an importing business to take the job would be an unacceptable conflict of interest. However, he could see no objection to taking a broader Finance portfolio ... Snookered, Hughes gave him the Treasury, effectively anointing him as his heir apparent.

His moment came with the 1922 election, which delivered the newly created Country Party the balance of power between the Nationalists and Labor. Its leader, Earle Page, refused to serve with Hughes, who was forced to hand the prime ministership to Bruce on what he hoped and believed would be a temporary basis. But Bruce again outguessed him by inviting Page into a formal coalition, the first since federation and the inauguration of an arrangement between the conservative parties which has endured ever since.

The government was to be known as the Bruce–Page government, with Page as deputy Prime Minister and the Country Party to hold five of the eleven cabinet positions. It was an extraordinarily generous offer that upset many Nationalists; after all, they had received more than three times as many votes as the Country Party but conceded nearly half of the executive positions. Bruce justified the deal by claiming that he was not governing just for his party, but for the nation: "we are not guided by ideological motives but by strict business principles," he proclaimed. Business principles became the hallmark of his government.

Unfortunately they did not prove adequate for an economy beset by foreign debt and rising unemployment. Some useful administrative reforms were made, including the establishment of a loans council and the use of section 96 of the constitution to make conditional grants to the states for special purposes, instead of simply handing over the money. But the situation continued to deteriorate. Bruce's own behaviour did not help; while insisting that the workers should accept massive wage cuts, he built his family a sixteen-room mansion in Frankston and was most often seen undertaking the leisurely pursuits of golf, horse riding and motoring.

Parliament sat seldom; Bruce preferred to govern by executive fiat. He made no apology for doing so: "If in a democracy you have the good fortune to get a Prime Minister of the capacity to be the kind of leader that almost approaches the point of being a dictator, it's incomparably the best form of government," he told his biographer. Of course, he added, you could always be sacked at the next general election. It was an option the voters did not pick up for another five years.

Bruce won the 1925 election on the slogan of "Sanity, Safety, Stability", and in the process launched what was to become one of the great stalwarts of conservative politics: the red menace. The unions, he averred, were in the grip of foreign agitators, socialist fanatics bent on destroying our way of life, "wreckers who would plunge us into the chaos and misery of class war". In 1926 he made strike action illegal and passed legislation to deport the dreaded insurgents, but unfortunately none could be located. The voters bought it once, but when he gave the scare another run in 1928, with unemployment nudging 12 per cent, they were less convinced. He scraped back with a reduced majority, but clearly more drastic action was required.

In an act of political bravado, Bruce moved to abolish the Commonwealth Arbitration Commission and hand back industrial relations to the states. Not only did this involve tearing up one of the covenants of federation; it also contradicted Bruce's previous policy, which had been to strengthen the powers of the commission. Having failed to do this, he now proposed to go to the other extreme. Confusion reigned and Hughes grabbed the opportunity to lead a small group of Nationalist rebels to vote against the new policy. The government fell, and at the subsequent election of 1929 Bruce lost his seat and, with it, all enthusiasm for the job.

He won the seat back in 1931, but working under Joe Lyons held no appeal; in any case, he was by now spending most of his time in London. Lyons, keen to retain his services in any capacity, asked Bruce to perform the duties of Australian high commissioner. In 1933 the position was formalised and Bruce resigned from parliament altogether. He remained high commissioner until 1945. He was offered a chance to return to Australia in 1938 to succeed the ailing Lyons, but he was not particularly keen and the prospect eventually fizzled out.

He later explained his feelings: "To face high office, e.g. a prime ministership, with any feeling other than that it is a wearisome burden, one must either glory in the position and the prestige that it brings … or be so convinced that one is so outstanding in ability and capacity that it is a blessing unto the people that one is at the head of their affairs. With regard to the first, while no doubt one's vanity would be greatly tickled by so great a position as that of Prime Minister of Great Britain I found such prestige as being Prime Minister of Australia gave one, made little appeal to me."

This, of course, was the point: Australia was always second best, if that. England was the real thing. At a time when the other dominions – Canada, South Africa – were seeking more independence from the mother country, Bruce's policy was always to cuddle up more closely. Undoubtedly the climax of his career was his elevation to the House of Lords in 1947, when he became the first Australian to take a seat in that chamber. He listed as his three greatest achievements his Cambridge blue, his captaincy of St Andrews Golf Club and his membership of the Royal Society. Australia still didn't rate: in 1951 Robert Menzies appointed him as the first chancellor of the Australian National University, but he visited it rarely and only for ceremonial occasions.

When Lord Bruce of Melbourne died in London in 1967, his middle name, which he took for his peerage, was his only serious remaining connection with the land of his birth. The radical nationalist Frank Anstey summed it up neatly: "Bruce was an Englishman born in Australia as some Englishmen are born in Delhi or Timbuctoo." Of all our prime ministers, he was the most accidental.

JAMES HENRY SCULLIN

Some politicians are just plain unlucky.

When Jimmy Scullin woke up on the morning of 20 October 1929 he must have thought he had the world at his feet. The election results were in: the ultra-conservative government of Stanley Bruce was routed, with Bruce himself thrown out of his seat. A cheering crowd saw the railway worker's son depart from Spencer Street station in Melbourne to take up his post in Canberra as Australia's ninth Prime Minister, with a sweeping mandate for change.

True, there were problems. Labor had been out of power for thirteen years and none of Scullin's new team had ministerial experience at the federal level. The conservatives still controlled the Senate and could be expected to resist the radical program Scullin had planned to revive the sagging economy. And sagging it was: for six years Bruce had tried to run the country in the same way he ran his import-export business, and had left a legacy of national debt and deficit and high unemployment.

Moreover the Labor Party was by no means united about the way forward; Scullin and his Treasurer, the former Queensland Premier Ted Theodore, had to steer a middle path between the right, led by Joseph Lyons, and the left, disciples of the NSW maverick Jack Lang. But Scullin had the respect of all factions. His dedication and integrity was beyond question. The first Labor Prime Minister to have been born in Australia (and also the first Catholic in the job) was entitled to feel cautiously confident as he and his wife Sarah boarded the train.

Within days came the news that the Wall Street market in New York had crashed, heralding the collapse of not only the Australian economy, but of the entire capitalist world. The story of Scullin's brief time in office is the story of his heroic but ultimately futile attempts to hold back the tsunami. Fortuitously, he was himself the child of a previous great depression.

James Henry Scullin was the fifth of eight children of Irish immigrants. He was born in 1876 at a railway siding at Trawalla, near Ballarat, and left the local state school at around the age of twelve to work at itinerant jobs; at various times through his teens he was farmhand, axeman and miner. He was described as a short and wiry man, who neither smoked nor drank – something of an ascetic. The depression of the 1890s hit his family hard and gave him a passion for social reform and justice, together with a hatred of oppression and a commitment to its victims.

In 1900 he moved to Ballarat, where he opened a grocery store and joined the burgeoning Labor movement. In 1906 he had the temerity to stand against the local member, the Prime Minister Alfred Deakin, and was soundly defeated.

He spent the next few years as an organiser for the Australian Workers' Union before being returned as the member for Corangamite in Andrew Fisher's 1910 victory. He lost his seat in 1913 but was by now a confident and compelling public speaker, and a prominent figure at Labor Party conferences. In 1916 he moved for the expulsion of Billy Hughes and his renegades and in 1921 was instrumental in the adoption of the socialist objective in Labor's platform. But he was never a revolutionary; his innate caution led him to work for change within the system rather than for its overthrow.

He won the seat of Yarra in 1922, and back in parliament he railed against Bruce's pro-business approach to government and his attempts to weaken the union movement. Presciently, he vehemently opposed the removal of the Commonwealth Bank from ministerial oversight; Bruce effectively made it independent of the government. In 1927 Scullin became deputy leader of his party and in 1928 succeeded Matthew Charlton in the leadership. Labor made useful gains in the 1928 election and gained power in the 1929 landslide. Then came the crash.

Orthodox economics counselled cutting expenditure and making the repayment of debts the top priority. Scullin and Theodore, anticipating John Maynard Keynes, favoured mildly expansionary policies. They were able to negotiate small rises in some social security benefits, some increases in tariffs, the removal of Australia from the gold standard and a reduction in assisted immigration. But that was where it ended. The chairman of the Commonwealth Bank board, the crusty and intransigent Sir Robert Gibson, refused to issue further credit unless the government agreed to cut pensions – which it would not do. Nor could it legislate for changes: the Senate was implacably hostile.

To make things still worse Scullin lost his right-hand man: Theodore was accused of having profited from the Queensland government's purchase of Mungana mines during his time as Premier and was forced to resign as Treasurer. Scullin took the portfolio himself, adding to his already overwhelming workload. In 1930 he was forced by political pressure to agree to a mission led by Sir Otto Niemeyer of the Bank of England to examine his country's finances. Niemeyer, satirised by local cartoonists as "Mr Moneybags", was mainly interested in protecting the profits of British bondholders – a stance which was enthusiastically supported by a young Nationalist lawyer named Robert Menzies.

Niemeyer's prescription for the crisis was simple: cut wages, repay debts, and under no circumstances spend money on public works to create jobs for the army of unemployed. That money should be reserved for the British bondholders. Scullin gave in on the need for both the Commonwealth and the states to try to rebalance their budgets but was otherwise unmoved, refusing to commit to specific cuts.

In response to Niemeyer he made a visit of his own: to the Imperial Conference in London. There he was able to persuade the British government not to drop its trade preferences for the Commonwealth (this was particularly important for Australian exports of wine, dried fruits and sugar) and to reduce Australia's annual interest payments on its debt by 1.6 million pounds – both significant wins.

But his visit is best remembered for his efforts in persuading King George V to accept Sir Isaac Isaacs as Australia's Governor-General. This post had previously been reserved for worthy upper-class military types or aristocratic nonentities whose influential relatives wanted them out of the country; it was particularly favoured for dissolute scions of noble families who appeared to have lost their chins in unfortunate breeding accidents.

Isaacs was a significant departure from the norm. He was a former chief justice, a jurist of great talent and achievement, a public figure of impeccable behaviour and standing. But he was also an Australian-born Jew. The King dug his heels in and Scullin insisted on a personal audience at Buckingham Palace. According to the historian Manning Clark it went like this:

They met at Buckingham Palace on 29 November, only a few hours after Jimmy Scullin had bade an emotional farewell to his relatives in the village of Ballyscullin. The King said he wanted to say something to the Australian Prime Minister: "We have sent many governors, Commonwealth and state, and I hope they have not all been failures." Scullin said no, they had not all been failures. He then unfolded his reasons why they had nominated an Australian. It was clear that he was not going to make any concessions.

This time the King-Emperor gave way. After explaining to Mr Scullin that the last thing he wanted was to be the centre of a public controversy, the King said: "I have been for 20 years a monarch and I hope I have always been a constitutional one, and being a constitutional monarch I must, Mr Scullin, accept your advice which, I take it, you will tender me formally by letter."

It was a huge symbolic win for Australian nationalism, and appreciated as such by the public. The opposition, led by John Latham, inveighed against it as being anti-British, but

Scullin revealed he had been prepared to fight a referendum and an election on the issue of whether an Australian was to be barred from the office of Governor-General. He could be determined when he wanted to be, and he showed this resolve again when he returned to Australia. His first act was to insist that Theodore, who had not yet been cleared of the charges against him (his "not guilty" verdict came later that year), be reinstated as Treasurer.

James Fenton and Joe Lyons, who had been acting Prime Minister and acting Treasurer in Scullin's absence, immediately resigned from the cabinet in protest and henceforth voted with the opposition. A supporter of Jack Lang's, Eddie Ward, then won a federal by-election: Scullin barred him from the party room because he had rejected the government's economic policy as part of his campaign. The Langites, led by "Stabber Jack" Beasley, solidified as a rebel group opposed to Scullin. He was now effectively in minority government with a hostile Senate.

He was clearly on borrowed time, but he managed to survive until the premiers' conference of mid-1931 at which the hostile groups somehow managed to agree to restructure public finances on what was called the "equality of sacrifice" principle. Everybody gave ground: resident bondholders accepted a 22.5 per cent cut in their interest while all governments agreed to a 20 per cent reduction in their expenditure. Scullin's caucus was still bitterly divided but the Nationalist opposition accepted the package and it went through the Senate. Keynes was to say later that the plan saved the economic structure of Australia.

But it could not save Scullin. A few months later his enemies combined to force him out of office. In the election that followed Labor was reduced to just 14 seats in a house of 75. He had done his best – a conservative government would almost certainly have made things even worse. But the pain had been too great. Ironically, Stanley Bruce regained his seat while Theodore, along with John Curtin and Ben Chifley, the young hopes of the party, all lost theirs.

Scullin stayed on as leader and regained some ground in the 1934 election, but in 1935 handed over to a re-elected Curtin. His health, never robust, was finally giving way; he had lost a kidney in his labouring days and needed more rest than a frontbench job allowed. And he wanted more time for himself. In a public display of restraint he had never moved into the Lodge, living instead in a modest hotel. His only known relaxations were an occasional game of lawn bowls and playing the violin in duets with his wife – they had no children.

But he remained in parliament on the backbench. When Labor regained office in 1941, he became a grey eminence consulted by the leadership on all matters of importance. There is a story that early in the life of the government Chifley dropped in to Curtin's office to find the Prime Minister and Scullin deep in conversation.

"Ah, Ben," said the party's elder statesman, "how is your health standing up?"

"Never better," replied Chifley.

"That's good," said Scullin. "It's got to be. I've got you down on my list for five portfolios already."

In later years Scullin took great interest in the Commonwealth Literary Fund and in the ABC, both of which he had planned to establish before his government was overtaken by events. He finally left parliament in 1949 and died just four years later. Under the circumstances it is hardly surprising that he left few legislative achievements behind him. But one which is frequently forgotten is the 1931 establishment of the Arnhem Land Reserve in the Northern Territory. The land was given to Aboriginal people to enable those who wished to do so to live a traditional lifestyle and preserve their culture without interference from whites.

A modest step, but in those days a radical one. It bears out the creed which is engraved on his tombstone: "Justice and humanity demand interference whenever the weak are being crushed by the strong."

JOSEPH ALOYSIUS LYONS

JOE LYONS IS remembered, when he is remembered at all, as the second of the great Labor rats – even more despised than the first because while Billy Hughes was thrown out, Lyons walked voluntarily, enticed by the blandishments of the enemy.

He was responsible for no ground-breaking legislation, made no memorable speeches and by all accounts was a singularly colourless individual: the cartoonists saw him as a cuddly but sleepy koala. He was intended as a stop-gap Prime Minister, a token conservative Catholic to break Labor's monopoly over his co-religionists; the idea was that he would bring victory in the 1931 election and then be replaced by a genuine, born-to-rule Tory.

But his prime ministership lasted nearly as long as the then record term of Hughes, and he was the first to win three successive elections. When he set another benchmark by becoming the first Prime Minister to die in office, the party which had sought to use him as a mere figurehead promptly disintegrated. He must have had something going for him.

Joseph Aloysius Lyons was born in Stanley, Tasmania, in 1879. His childhood was a tough one; his father lost the family savings betting on the 1887 Melbourne Cup and at the age of nine young Joseph was put to work, first as an errand boy and then as a farm labourer. When he turned twelve he was rescued by two aunts, who sent him back to school and encouraged him to take up a career as a teacher. He had a rebellious streak and clashed frequently with the state Education Department. The tensions were exacerbated when he joined the Tasmanian ALP. But his amiable and avuncular appearance helped to disarm his opponents.

Having moved to Launceston, he stood for state parliament in 1909 and ran a vigorous campaign in the course of which he was publicly horsewhipped by an enraged landowner. He later attributed his victory to that incident. He rose rapidly through the ranks of the parliamentary party and by 1912 was president of the state branch. When Labor gained power in 1914 Lyons was Deputy Premier, Treasurer, and Minister for Railways and for Education. He was clearly a man on his way up.

But there was a problem. In 1913 he had become "enamoured", as contemporary accounts have it, of a fifteen-year-old schoolgirl named Enid Burnell. The relationship was clearly an uneven one, and remained so when the two were married two years later: Enid, seventeen, was a trainee teacher and Joseph, thirty-five, as Education Minister, was technically her employer. Even in Tasmania it was something of a scandal. But it was apparently a genuine love match, resulting in eleven children and a formidable political partnership to boot. There is some argument about the extent of Enid's influence and ambition, but she was a tireless campaigner; in the 1925 state election both she and her mother stood as Labor candidates, more to split the opposition vote than with any hope of winning. Enid eventually entered federal parliament, as a widow, to become Australia's first female minister.

But this was a long way in the future. Lyons had become Premier of Tasmania in 1923 and held the job until Labor lost the election of 1928. But he was no longer content either with opposition or with state politics. He became part of Jimmy Scullin's federal team for the 1929 election on the understanding that he would be given a cabinet post if he won, and Scullin kept the promise and made him Postmaster-General. It was not the portfolio he wanted. Lyons felt that his state Treasury experience had entitled him to be Treasurer, a job held by "Red Ted" Theodore, whose radical notions Lyons distrusted.

When Theodore was forced to stand down over the Mungana mines affair, Scullin took the job for himself; however, Lyons acted in the portfolio in 1930 while Scullin was overseas and was generally believed to have done so successfully. He fully expected to be confirmed in the job when Scullin returned. Instead, the embattled Prime Minister reinstated Theodore.

Outraged, Lyons retired to the backbench and was immediately identified as a potential recruit by the opposition Nationalist Party, then led by the hard-line conservative John Latham, who was persuaded that he would have to stand aside – at least temporarily – if Lyons could be enticed to defect. Lyons soon found himself being duchessed by an influential clique of Melbourne citizens who became known as the Savage Group, after their preferred meeting place, the Savage Club. As well as prominent businessmen, the Group included the young Robert Menzies, seen as a rising star of conservative politics.

Lyons was induced to join the United Australia Movement, an ostensibly non-political but avowedly conservative organisation which eventually morphed into the United Australia Party. Lyons was already a popular public figure and became much better known when the press baron Keith Murdoch launched a campaign to promote him. He was paraded as a "no-party" leader, a man whose loyalty was to the people, whose appeal crossed traditional party lines and political affiliations.

Even the fiery socialist Mary Gilmore was seduced. In a letter to Enid after Lyons's death she wrote: "I would still feel I voted Labor if I voted for him ... his heart was with the people." Greeted by a cheering crowd in Adelaide, Lyons added a quasi-religious note to the proceedings: "We shall strike a match tonight that will start a blaze throughout Australia." In 1931 he became the official leader of the UAP and therefore of the opposition.

Already battered by trying to ride out the Great Depression and crippled by divisions within his own party, Scullin had no defence against the crusade. The UAP won the 1931 election in a landslide; Lyons did not need the Country Party to form a coalition government with him. Despite opposition from the relentlessly sectarian Protestants in his party, Lyons had time to consolidate his leadership and proved a masterful negotiator.

Indeed, some saw him as too flexible and ready to

compromise; there were times when he appeared to respond to the slightest pressure from interest groups. There were constant rumours that he would face a challenge in the party room; ministers and backbenchers alike complained that it was a do-nothing government, content to coast along on the tide of the recovering economy without purpose or direction. But Lyons's popularity with the general public proved undiminished. Air travel had now come to Australia and Lyons, together with his wife, barnstormed the country on a regular basis.

He was the first politician to exploit the possibilities of the new medium, radio. Traditional campaigning was still done at public meetings, with all the attendant risks of heckling and disruption; Lyons instead retired to radio studios to put his message without fear of interruption, most especially to the country's housewives. Honest Joe Lyons, the family man. It was a brilliantly successful tactic: his government was returned in 1934, although he was forced back into coalition with the Country Party, and Lyons won a record third term against a resurgent Labor Party, led by John Curtin, in 1937.

But times were changing. The fascist regimes were rampant in Europe and war appeared probable. Lyons, a lifelong pacifist, became a determined appeaser. During one overseas trip he actually called on Benito Mussolini to assure him of Australia's friendship and he publicly supported giving the Sudetenland to Germany if it would satisfy Hitler's demands.

At the same time his hold on his own party was becoming tenuous; Enid warned him that Menzies, who had gone to the backbench after a cabinet dispute, was openly undermining him, but he was too tired – or too fed up – to care.

By the end of 1938 he was ready to hand over, but not to Menzies; he made one last approach to Bruce, who he had always hoped could be tempted home to succeed him, but could not meet the conditions Bruce demanded. On a train trip to Sydney in 1939 he suffered a heart attack and died in hospital, appropriately for a devout Catholic, on Good Friday.

Menzies, the direct beneficiary of his death, was generous, describing Lyons as brave, strong and adroit. Bruce was less kind: "Joe Lyons was a delightful person. He couldn't run a government but he could win elections." This was precisely the reason the conservatives had made him their leader. They had needed a popular, compliant figurehead to take them into government and Joe Lyons had answered the call. Honest Joe Lyons delivered on the deal. Not such a bad epitaph after all.

EARLE CHRISTMAS GRAFTON **PAGE**

EARLE CHRISTMAS GRAFTON Page was indeed born in Grafton, but not on 25 December; the date was 8 August 1880 and he was not six weeks premature, either. His name was not the only contrary aspect of his life. A brilliant surgeon, successful businessman and ruthless bargainer, he was nonetheless a failure as a politician.

His period as Treasurer resulted in debt, deficit and unemployment, leaving Australia singularly ill-equipped to handle the Great Depression that followed it. The National Health Act he believed would be his lasting monument did indeed, as he boasted, "provide a bulwark against the socialisation of medicine", but it did so by privileging doctors at the expense of patients and debilitating the public hospital system. And his short tenure as stop-gap Prime Minister was one of the most divisive in Australian political history, splitting his party and destabilising the government that followed it.

But for all that he left one undeniable legacy: it was Page, more than any other figure, who set the ground rules for the longstanding alliance between the rural and urban conservatives that has preserved the Country Party (now the Nationals) as one of the world's most enduring and effective agrarian forces.

Page's father lost his money in the 1890s depression, but the young Earle Page was able to secure scholarships to Sydney Boys High and Sydney University, where he entered medical school at the extraordinarily young age of fifteen and graduated in 1902. After a period as house surgeon at Royal Prince Alfred Hospital he returned to Grafton and quickly became proprietor of a thriving private hospital, as well as the surgeon of choice for the surrounding 10,000 square miles.

He acquired several dairy farms and a sawmill and joined the local Farmers and Settlers' Association. He was prominent in the northern NSW New State movement and in 1913 was elected to Grafton Council and bought a controlling share in the local newspaper. It was a promising platform from which to launch a political career.

However, war interrupted; Page joined the AIF Medical Corps and served in Egypt and France. In 1917 he applied for, and was granted, repatriation and ignored all subsequent orders to report back to Sydney for military duties. He did, however, take an active part in recruitment campaigns, which, together with his business connections, saved him from disciplinary action. In 1919 he won the seat of Cowper and promptly joined the newly formed Country Party. A year later he was elected deputy leader and the year after that took the leadership.

He immediately flexed his new-found political muscle. The ruling Nationalists under Billy Hughes were by now a divided and struggling minority government, dependent on the support of the Country Party and independents. Page offered them permanent coalition in return for the removal of Hughes (whom he described as "a fig-leaf socialist") as leader, the deputy prime ministership and Treasury portfolio for himself, and five of the eleven cabinet positions for his party. It was an outrageous demand, but it worked. The government that took office for the next seven years was known not as the Bruce government but as the Bruce–Page government.

When it fell in 1929 the new Nationalist leader, John Latham, sought to maintain some sort of coalition in opposition but Page would not agree to his terms, although he did offer himself as minister in any subsequent conservative government. This time he outsmarted himself: in 1931 the UAP under Joe Lyons won a majority in its own right and Page's services were not required. However his period on the sideline was spent in considerable comfort; now a very rich man, Page saw off the Depression with equanimity.

When the coalition was reinstated after the 1934 election, it was on terms far less favourable to the Country Party, which was henceforth kept firmly in its place as the junior partner. One of those determined that this should be the case was Robert Menzies, who now replaced Hughes as the principal target of Page's not inconsiderable spleen. Page spent a lot of effort in trying to persuade Stanley Bruce to return from London and thus thwart Menzies's obvious leadership ambition, but in vain.

When Lyons died in 1939, Menzies, who despite having resigned as Attorney-General over a disagreement about national insurance policy was still technically the UAP's deputy leader, should have been his automatic successor as

PM. Instead Page, who had been Lyons's deputy Prime Minister, advised the Governor-General to grant him the commission, promising to resign as soon as a new UAP leader could be elected. But he added a rider: he would not serve under Menzies. This time his bluff was called. Menzies was elected as the UAP leader, and therefore Prime Minister, and Page's nineteen days of power came to an end.

When parliament resumed he made a swingeing attack on his conqueror, saying that Menzies's public record did not suggest that he had the right qualifications for the job. Three incidents, he said, "give me no basis of confidence that he possesses the maximum courage or loyalty or judgement". The three incidents were Menzies's resignation from cabinet when the country was preparing for war, a speech on leadership which was widely taken as an attack on Lyons, and the fact that in 1915 Menzies had resigned his military commission and not seen overseas service.

Page's tirade was greeted with uproar in the house; next day the *Sydney Morning Herald* described the speech as "a violation of the decencies of debate without parallel in the annals of the federal parliament". The Country Party split, with Arthur Fadden leading three other members out of the party room. However, neither Country Party group was prepared to support a vote of "no confidence" so the UAP was able to continue as a minority government.

Five months later, with the outbreak of World War II Page attempted a comeback; he was now prepared to form a coalition but Menzies would agree only if he, not Page, could select the entire ministry. Page insisted that he should choose the Country Party ministers, and the agreement fell through. He was forced to resign as party leader and was replaced by

Archie Cameron, with Fadden's group returning to the party. Menzies eventually offered a compromise and the coalition was restored, but with Page remaining on the backbench.

After the 1940 election the party leadership changed again: Cameron was challenged by John McEwen and when the vote was tied at eight all between Page and McEwen the party elected Arthur Fadden as a stop-gap; the stop-gap lasted eighteen years. Page returned to the ministry but in the comparatively junior portfolio of commerce. When Fadden had his own brief stint as Prime Minister he sent Page to London as Australia's special envoy to the war cabinet. John Curtin maintained him in that position until the end of the war.

He retained his seat of Cowper and when Menzies returned to office in 1949 became Minister for Health, a portfolio he held until he retired to the backbench in 1956. The national health insurance scheme he set up endured until 1974, when it was finally replaced by Gough Whitlam's Medibank after much kicking and screaming from the medical profession. In his latter years Page spent more time in his beloved Clarence Valley, still fervently advocating that the region be declared a separate state. It was a vigorous semi-retirement; until the age of eighty he remained an aggressive tennis player and a keen horseman.

His competitive urge never deserted him and he was spared the ignominy of a final defeat. In the election of 1961 he lost the seat of Cowper after holding it for forty-two years, but he died before the votes could be counted. He is remembered with some awe and considerable fondness in his home town of Grafton, the centre of the electorate which now bears his name.

ROBERT GORDON MENZIES

Most prime ministers have a term in office. Bob Menzies had an era.

In retrospect the Menzies years were like the stars in the sky – uncountable, unmoving. It was an age of stasis, when nothing ever seemed to change. Tennyson wrote of the land of the Lotos Eaters, "a land where it seemed always afternoon". It was perhaps no coincidence that Menzies chose to call his own memoir *Afternoon Light*.

Even those centres of ferment, the universities, succumbed. The students sang:

> There'll always be a Menzies
> While there's a BHP
> For they have drawn their dividends
> Since 1893.
>
> There'll always be a Menzies
> For Menzies never fails

As long as nothing happens to
The Bank of New South Wales.

If we should lose our Menzies
Wherever should we be
If Menzies means as much to you
As Menzies means to me.

It is worth noting that the two venerable institutions mentioned did not drag themselves into the modern world until the great man had retired.

When he finally left politics, celebrated by cheering masses and clanking with imperial honours, the first thought of many was that Australia could at last begin to catch up; the Menzies years had been relaxed and comfortable, but they had been largely a waste of time.

And yet: in his time in office, Menzies took Australia into three wars – four if you count the Malayan Emergency – and steered us through the most critical years of the Cold War, including our greatest spy story. In the process he weathered boom and bust, oversaw vast technological change (including, to his lasting distaste, the introduction of television), won eight elections, lost a referendum and saw off three opposition leaders and, perhaps more personally relevant, four Australian cricket captains.

The times were seldom dull: why, then, the impression that so little actually happened? It was partly the man's always calm and paternal presence: whether you liked his policies or not (or even cared if he had any), you knew somehow that Menzies would look after you. And you knew this because he did not tamper with the great verities of

Australian politics: White Australia, tariff protection, the industrial arbitration system, the welfare state and, most importantly – to him at least – the ties with Great Britain.

Menzies remained, he boasted, British to the bootstraps – this at a time when few Australians even knew that such accoutrements had once existed. It was a quaint and old-fashioned image but a strangely reassuring one.

Menzies was, of course, a product of the bootstrap age, born in 1894 in the small town of Jeparit in western Victoria. The son of a storekeeper who doubled as a Methodist lay preacher, from an early age he was instilled with the virtues of thrift, hard work, piety and patriotism. He was also well-groomed and serious – the seeds of the pomposity which characterised his later years were sown early. His education at Ballarat, Wesley College and Melbourne University revealed him as something of a student prodigy, but a sturdily conservative one: at university he undertook a first class honours law degree, but found time to become president of the Students' Representative Council and the Students' Christian Union, and to edit the Melbourne University magazine, which he turned into a patriotic tract pushing the cause of conscription in World War I.

But he did not himself enlist. While there were good family reasons for keeping one son out of the army, his failure to serve was forever held against him by his critics.

At the time, however, these were few and unimportant. The young Menzies was handsome, charming and witty, and quickly came to the notice of influential backers. Sir Owen Dixon took him as a pupil and he was marked down for advancement by the Tory war hero Sir Wilfrid Kent Hughes and the influential commentator Frederic Eggleston. In

1920, as a relative newcomer to the bar he won an important case in the High Court and not long afterwards became the youngest King's Counsel in the country.

He joined the Young Nationalists and rose to become their president, and in 1928 won a seat in the Victorian Legislative Council. In 1929 he exchanged it for a seat in the Assembly and when the Nationalists gained power in 1932 became state Attorney-General and Minister for Railways. He became a member of the Savage Group responsible for persuading Joe Lyons to defect from Labor, and in return Lyons asked him to move to federal politics, promising to make him Commonwealth Attorney-General (which he did) and to hand him the leadership before the 1937 election (which he didn't).

Menzies took the safe seat of Kooyong in a by-election in 1934 and held it for the next thirty-two years. He had already played a federal role from outside parliament; when Lyons was acting as Treasurer in 1930 he had defied caucus by refusing to defer the conversion of a Commonwealth loan and Menzies had helped him to re-float it.

The young lawyer had strong views on the subject; in a speech in 1931 he had insisted that the contracts requiring the payment of dividends to British bondholders be seen as sacrosanct, and honoured whatever the cost. "If Australia was to surmount her troubles only by abandonment of traditional British standards of honesty, justice, fair play and honest endeavour, it would be better for Australia that every citizen within her boundaries should die of starvation during the next six months," he thundered, in words which would be used against him for the rest of his career.

At the time they were regarded as clear evidence of a

selfish, uncaring and even unpatriotic attitude. Many of his parliamentary colleagues resented Menzies's air of superiority and he did little to placate them. In an altercation with the Country Party's pugnacious Archie Cameron, Menzies said coldly: "Archie, I do not suffer fools gladly." Cameron snapped back: "It might be news to you to know that bloody fools have a lot of trouble putting up with you, too."

Menzies never doubted his own ability and became increasingly impatient when Lyons hung on as Prime Minister during and after 1937. Lyons's original mentor, the publisher Keith Murdoch, agreed that his protégé had reached his use-by date and took up Menzies's cause. By now he was deputy leader and clearly the heir apparent, in spite of strong opposition from Earle Page's faction in the Country Party as well as some UAP members who believed he was disloyal to Lyons.

He was less popular with the public: when the wharfies refused to load pig-iron for Japan, claiming that it could be applied to make weapons for use against Australia in the war which was widely seen as inevitable, Menzies invoked the full force of industrial law against them. He was stuck forever with the sobriquet Pig-Iron Bob.

Eventually Menzies used a disagreement over national insurance as a pretext to resign from the ministry; but before the politics of this move could play out, Lyons solved the problem by dying. Against vehement protests by Page, the UAP elected Menzies as its new leader, and therefore Prime Minister.

One of his early duties was to announce that England had declared war on Germany, and that as a result, Australia was also at war. He appealed to the populace to behave normally.

Certainly the government showed little sense of urgency. National servicemen were called up, but not for overseas service. Recruitment for a second AIF was set in motion, and munitions factories prepared, but in the early days at least not much changed.

Menzies proposed a national, all-party government for the course of the conflict but Page would not serve in it and the Labor leader John Curtin also refused: he thought the war effort would be better pursued by a single, unified party in power, and in the 1940 election Labor fell just short of fulfilling that role. With Page replaced as leader, the Country Party rejoined the coalition, but even so Menzies had to depend on the votes of two independents.

It was hardly an opportune time for the Prime Minister to leave the country. Nonetheless Menzies did so, travelling via Canada to London, ostensibly to plead the case for the allies to pay more attention to Singapore, but also in the hope of being invited to join Winston Churchill's war cabinet. He failed in both endeavours and his party used his absence to decide that it could do without him. Incredibly, there was no challenger from within the majority UAP; it was prepared to hand the prime ministership to its junior partner simply to get rid of Menzies.

Although he had received warnings, notably from Percy Spender, that his political grave was being dug, Menzies had ignored them, and made what he thought was a triumphal return to Sydney. But when he reached Canberra he realised that it was all over. He resigned and left the party room in tears, murmuring to his private secretary, Cecil Looker: "I have been done. I'll lie down and bleed for a while."

Most of his colleagues thought his career was over but

Archie Cameron, who had now switched from the Country Party to the UAP, knew better. "Finished?" he barked. "He'll be back. The bloomin' big cow's only stepped off the road to clean the muck off his boots and cut himself a new waddy." And he had; but it was to be eight years before he was ready to wield it. They were not wasted years: Menzies used them to remake not only his side of Australian politics, but also his own persona. Labor decisively won the 1941 election and from opposition Menzies supported John Curtin and the war effort, while studiously cultivating that section of the community he was to christen "the forgotten people" – the socially conservative middle class who would provide the backbone of his support for more than two decades.

He did this through a series of radio broadcasts; he had admired Joe Lyons's mastery of the new medium and now he sought to emulate it. The weekly chats dealt with current affairs, but more specifically with the problems faced by households disrupted by the war. They were hugely successful. Menzies had deliberately bypassed the mainstream media, which were far more critical. Menzies disliked and avoided the press, later telling President Richard Nixon: "In all my life I have treated the press with marked contempt and remarkable success." (Nixon commented: "No one would ever forget Robert Menzies. I learned a lot from him.")

Largely as a result of the broadcasts, by 1943, when he was re-elected as leader of the UAP after its massive election defeat, the previously aloof Menzies was on his way to becoming a national father figure. Convincing his colleagues that the change was genuine was more difficult; a common complaint was that he still regarded himself as superior to any other politician, living or dead, and that he considered himself to be doing the nation a favour by deigning to lead it. Nonetheless they were desperate for someone to rescue them from the dire straits in which they now found themselves, and there were few complaints when Menzies announced that it was time to reform the remnants of the UAP into a new and more inclusive party – the Liberal Party.

He received immediate backing from the business-oriented Institute of Public Affairs, whose members were concerned that Labor would use the need for post-war reconstruction to introduce some form of socialism. The influential Victorian Charles Kemp produced a paper entitled "Looking Forward", which became the blueprint for the new party. The Melbourne *Argus* was an enthusiastic supporter of what it called the Menzies Party, and he was certainly its founder, policy-maker and undisputed leader.

Although he insisted that the Liberals were the party of middle Australia and had moved beyond class warfare, they were still regarded by many as the representatives of big business, which was, after all, their principal source of funds. Menzies had hoped that, following the death of the popular John Curtin, they could win the 1946 election; instead Ben Chifley led Labor to another comfortable victory. Menzies took the rejection hard and contemplated leaving politics altogether, but he was reinvigorated by Chifley's 1947 promise to nationalise the banks. The High Court eventually declared the policy unconstitutional, but it gave Menzies a platform for what he called a great new struggle for civic freedom.

Perhaps more important to the voters was his policy to end all war-time rationing. In coalition with the Country Party the Liberals swept to power in 1949 and the Menzies era began. In that election thirty-nine new Liberal members entered parliament; they owed their seats to Menzies and gave him an unassailable support base, so much so that he was never seriously challenged.

He had inherited from Chifley a dedicated and efficient public service, which he retained, despite the urgings of some to clean out the socialists. Menzies chose to accept that they would act with impartiality and integrity, and they did not let him down. This was of particular benefit in economic matters, where the Menzies team was comparatively weak. A pattern quickly developed: Menzies would call in such luminaries as Roland Wilson, Richard Randall and H.C. "Nugget" Coombs, and outline his plans for the next fiscal period. He would then look expectantly at the troops, one of whom would say: "Prime Minister, you have told us what you wish to do. We will now tell you what you are able to do." And they would, and he would do it.

But Menzies's great concern was communism – the Red Menace. He had seen the intensity of the Cold War at first hand during a trip to Europe in 1948 and became obsessed with the need to eradicate communism from Australia. In fact the party was very much a fringe group; the communists were influential in sections of the trades union movement but had virtually no popular support. Nonetheless Menzies moved to declare the party illegal. At first a hostile Senate stalled the legislation; after the double-dissolution election of 1951 it went through, but was declared unconstitutional by the High Court. Menzies took his crusade to the people by way of a referendum, but it was narrowly defeated.

A useful consequence of his obsession quickly emerged: deep divisions were developing within the Labor Party.

Chifley had died in 1951 and his successor, the brilliant but erratic Bert Evatt, was fighting to hold his troops together. The well-timed defection of a Soviet spy, Vladimir Petrov, in 1954 exacerbated the situation further. Evatt had hoped to win the 1954 election, but the Petrov affair, together with his rash and unfunded promises of handouts for all, led to another Menzies victory, albeit a narrow one. Menzies consolidated that win with a snap poll the next year in what was openly described as the "Crush Evatt" election.

Labor split, and following another defeat in 1958, Evatt retired, a broken man, to become chief justice of New South Wales. Menzies had seen off his oldest and most hated enemy; even his friends admitted that he had always envied Evatt's superior legal brain. But in politics Evatt was no match for the master, who was now known as "Ming the Merciless" after an ill-advised attempt to have his name given the Scottish pronunciation of "Minghis"; Australians felt he had more in common with the super-villain of the *Flash Gordon* comics.

He had another close shave after the credit squeeze of 1961, when his government hung on by a single seat after a diligent campaign by Arthur Calwell.

But again he was able to consolidate in 1963. His leadership was never in doubt: occasionally a potential rival put his head up, but Menzies promptly moved him out of parliament to some other prestigious post. Such was the fate of Richard Casey, Percy Spender and Garfield Barwick. So the Menzies government was pretty much a one-man band, with a number of capable lieutenants in Paul Hasluck, Allen Fairhall, Harold Holt and other lesser lights, but no obvious replacements. He was also aided by strong Country Party leaders in Arthur

Fadden and John McEwen, and placed great stress on maintaining the coalition as his top political priority.

That, and the creation of the Liberal Party, he regarded as his greatest achievements. His supporters would add the massive expansion of the university system and education in general (it was Menzies who introduced state aid to church schools) and the development of the city of Canberra. But they would be hard-pressed to point to much else. The Menzies years were comfortable and generally prosperous as Australia rode the post-war boom, but they could not be described as years of innovation and reform. This was how Menzies wanted it: although he insisted on describing himself as a true liberal, his instincts were deeply conservative.

This was clear from his forays into foreign affairs. He travelled regularly to London for the British Commonwealth prime ministers' conference, extending his stay if it happened to be an Ashes cricket tour year, but he became alarmed at the increasing presence of post-colonial prime ministers from Africa and Asia. A devoted upholder of the White Australia policy, Menzies was never really comfortable with other races or cultures; he was humiliated by Egypt's President Nasser, who christened him "The Bushman" when he ill-advisedly accepted a role as mediator in the 1956 Suez crisis, and he was publicly snubbed by India's Prime Minister, Jawaharlal Nehru. In 1961 he defended South Africa's right to remain in the Commonwealth despite its policy of apartheid, and when the country finally resigned he complained that it had been "pushed out".

He had no hesitation in exploiting Australians' traditional fear of Asia to win votes; in the Menzies years the Yellow Peril joined the Red Menace as a threat to our way of life.

In the Vietnam War, the two merged wonderfully into a kind of Orange Bogeyman. Then, as with Korea and the Cold War, Menzies never questioned the American alliance. But his real love was always England, and he yearned for the trappings of the vanishing empire. His devotion to royalty was unstinting: his embarrassing quotation of Robert Ford's mawkish poem ("I did but see her passing by / And yet I love her till I die") at a banquet for Queen Elizabeth II was matched only by his last-ditch attempt to have Australia's decimal currency unit named the Royal rather that the Dollar.

He rejoiced in the glittering prizes he received in return for his loyalty. His elevation as a Knight of the Order of the Thistle was greeted by Australians with subdued amusement but there was open derision when he was created Lord Warden of the Cinque Ports, with an absurd uniform, part-ownership of a castle built for Henry VIII and the untrammelled right to salvage flotsam and jetsam from a large section of the south coast of England. For all his political skills, Sir Robert Gordon Menzies never developed the common touch. Nonetheless on his retirement on Australia Day 1966 he was farewelled with widespread applause, even if it was the kind of applause given to a great performer's final bow rather than a tribute to a loved and revered statesman.

He chose his own time, and all but disappeared into a quiet retirement spent largely at his home in Melbourne, where he died in 1978. He left few monuments, but at his birthplace of Jeparit the citizens have erected one: a concrete thistle atop a column. With typical Australian irreverence, it is known locally as "Ming's pisspot". The Lord Warden would not have been amused.

ARTHUR WILLIAM FADDEN

ARTIE FADDEN REALLY should have joined the Labor Party.

Born in 1895, the son of Irish immigrants who settled in Ingham, North Queensland, he started working life as a canecutter before graduating to office work and reaching the giddy heights of appointment as town clerk of Mackay. His upward social mobility did not stop there; a gregarious and amiable man, he attracted the attention of the local landholders and was lured into the rural organisations which gave birth to the Country Party.

In 1930 he stood successfully for the Townsville Council, and in 1932 moved to the state Legislative Assembly, albeit as an opposition backbencher.

He lost his seat in the Labor landslide of 1935 but by then had developed a taste for politics, a craft which seemed to come naturally to him. A year later he won the seat of Darling Downs in a by-election and Arthur William Fadden was on his way to Canberra.

The Lyons–Page coalition was still in government, but the Country Party had lost the clout Earle Page had given it in its early days, and Fadden was not considered for a ministry. Nonetheless he became a central figure in the party room and when Lyons died in 1939 had a small but significant following of his own. He showed his muscle when Page, with whom he had never got on, attempted to veto Menzies as Lyons's successor and made a savage attack on Menzies's character in parliament. Fadden and three others walked out of the party meeting, although they retained their party membership.

The rift remained when Archie Cameron took over the party leadership, but Menzies reformed the coalition and Fadden became an assistant minister. After a plane crash killed three members of cabinet, he was made Minister for Air and Civil Aviation, and after the 1940 election was Treasurer, a portfolio from which he was to deliver a record eleven budgets.

The leadership struggles within the Country Party continued, with Cameron, Page and John McEwen contesting the position in 1941. Cameron withdrew, and the other two were locked in a tied vote; Fadden was made acting leader while the impasse was sorted out. But before that could happen the UAP deposed Menzies as its leader. The coalition government was hanging on with the support of two independents, and the Country Party threatened to withdraw unless Fadden, who had acted as Prime Minister while Menzies was overseas, was confirmed in the position. The UAP folded and Fadden was launched on his forty days of power.

Unsurprisingly, nothing of significance was achieved, and Labor, unified and ready to govern, pounced: the independents were persuaded to vote for a "no confidence" motion. As Fadden recalled it, John Curtin broke the news. "On the day the vote was to be taken Curtin called on me on his way to lunch. 'Well, boy,' he said, 'have you got the numbers? I hope you have but I don't think you have.' I replied, 'No, John, I haven't got them. I have heard that Wilson spent the weekend at Evatt's place and I can't rely on Coles.' Curtin said, 'Well, there it is. Politics is a funny game.' Wryly I replied, 'Yes, but there's no need for them to make it any funnier.'"

Curtin became Prime Minister and was confirmed with a landslide win in 1943, which effectively wiped out the UAP. Fadden had remained as opposition leader – Hughes had been re-elected leader of the UAP. But the coalition was on the point of collapse, especially after Menzies made a speech disowning much of Fadden's policy on the eve of the election; Fadden complained that he had been "stabbed in the back".

The two men were never close, but when Menzies formed the Liberal Party he persuaded Fadden to bring the Country Party into a new coalition, and things improved considerably after the pair won government in 1949. In a way they were a natural fit: the urbane, aloof Prime Minister and his brash, knockabout deputy. The combination worked particularly well in the Red Menace elections of the 1950s, when Menzies took the high ground while Fadden smeared the Labor Party with guilt by association.

In spite of this, he was generally well liked and could take a joke against himself. He was fond of telling the story of a campaign meeting in 1951. A heckler had asked him: "Why don't you lazy politicians who live off us do a fair day's work?" Fadden went on: "There was loud laughter from the hall. I moved to the front of the platform and shouted back, 'Look, my non-musical friend, I work while you're asleep.' A voice came from the other side of the hall, 'Of course you do. We all know you're a burglar.'"

He was cast in that light in 1951–52, when the wool boom forced him to bring down a horror budget to control inflation. He became temporarily so unpopular that he said "I could have had a meeting of all my friends and supporters in a one-man telephone booth." It was probably this experience that led to his establishment of the Reserve Bank to control interest rates, his most enduring legacy.

He retired in 1958 in the hope that he would be rewarded with the chairmanship of the Commonwealth Banking Corporation, which he had strengthened and reformed, but he had to be content with a knighthood. He remained active in the Country Party, resisting John McEwen's attempts to broaden its base to include urban electorates; until his death in 1973 he believed the party could only succeed by representing rural interests against those of the cities.

Even in retirement, he was always ready with a piece of useful advice. Perhaps the most memorable was: "When you're over the age of forty, never go past a lift or a lavatory."

JOHN JOSEPH **CURTIN**

THERE IS NO doubting John Curtin's stature in Australian history.

Many, including his contemporary opponent Arthur Fadden, and his Labor successor Bob Hawke, rate him the greatest of Australia's Prime Ministers. Others point to the magnitude of the task he undertook as leader on the first occasion Australia's shores were threatened and the courage with which he took the distasteful and often unpopular decisions he regarded as necessary for Australians' protection.

And all acknowledge the scale of his personal tragedy: the man of peace condemned to conduct a war, who died as the hard-fought victory was finally in sight. In his country's brief history he was a hero of Shakespearean proportions, a man driven by circumstance to a destiny he neither foresaw nor desired.

John Joseph Ambrose Curtin was born in the Victorian village of Creswick in 1885. His father, an Irish immigrant, worked variously as a soldier, policeman, prison warden and publican, but by the time the family finally settled in the Melbourne suburb of Brunswick, Curtin's mother had become a seamstress to support the family.

John was educated in various two-room Catholic schools and at one time his dedication and earnestness marked him as a potential priest, but he was forced to enter the workforce at the age of ten as a messenger boy, including a stint at the *Age,* where he gained a taste for journalism. He held a number of unskilled jobs and played cricket and football at a respectable level, but most of his spare time was spent at the public library where he pursued his education. This led him to a clerk's job with the Titan Manufacturing Company, where he joined the union and swapped his religious faith for a zealous brand of socialism.

He came under the wing of the firebrand politician Frank Anstey, and took up street-corner oratory on behalf of the revolutionary Victorian Socialist Party, becoming a frequent contributor to its propaganda sheets. It was an exciting and hectic lifestyle, and as a result Curtin became a heavy drinker, a problem which was to continue for much of his career.

By 1910 the VSP had largely unravelled, but Curtin, still a revolutionary socialist, was firmly ensconced in the union movement. Next year he took up a full-time job as secretary of the Timber Workers' Union and in 1914 became its president. He also stood unsuccessfully for the federal seat of Balaclava. After a brief vacation, some of which he spent drying out in a private hospital, Curtin re-emerged as an organiser for the Australian Workers' Union and soon afterwards was appointed secretary of the union movement's anti-conscription campaign, a job he filled with such enthusiasm that he was arrested on a charge of failing to enlist and served three days in jail before the charge was withdrawn. However, the campaign was successful and the Prime Minister, Billy Hughes, split the Labor Party and was expelled from it.

Curtin, exhausted and debilitated, sought a fresh start and found one in the west; he was offered the editorship of the *Westralian Worker* and moved to Perth. His fiancée, Elsie Needham, joined him and they were married in 1917. The change to a more stable existence worked; he even gave up the grog for the first time. And his political values began to moderate. While he still yearned to see an Australia that was "a republic of the discontented peoples of the earth", he became increasingly drawn to the idea of parliamentary reform through the Labor Party.

He again stood unsuccessfully for federal parliament in 1919, the year of the conservative backlash. In 1924 he was sent to Geneva as the Australian delegate to the International Labour Organization convention. He also visited Paris and London, and met many of the leading lights of the left. The experience finally convinced him that "the opportunity for overthrowing capitalism has passed – Labor governments are the hope of the world." From that time his commitment to the ALP was unquestioned.

In 1928 he finally won the seat of Fremantle, but was not included in Jim Scullin's ministry, an exclusion he thought unjust. But throughout Labor's brief and stormy term in office he was prominent on the backbench, among other things leading the charge to expel the rebel supporters of NSW Premier Jack Lang. But he was now back on the booze and, on losing his seat in Labor's landslide defeat of 1931, suffered a breakdown. When he recovered, he again swore off the grog, this time for good.

But it was still on his colleagues' minds when he regained his seat in 1934 and returned to Canberra and a party looking for a leader to succeed the failing Scullin. Curtin was approached by the party elder E.J. Holloway. "Do you have it conquered, Jack?" Holloway asked.

"Yes," he replied.

"I have been asked by the Party to invite you to stand for an important position."

"What is it?"

"The chaps want me to guarantee you will keep sober."

"Of course I would – what is the position?"

"Leader of the Party."

"Me! Not me – I wouldn't have a chance."

"Oh yes, you would. I have a team prepared to vote for you if you pass on your promise that you have given up the drink."

"You tell them – I promise and I will carry out my promise."

In 1935 Curtin was elected leader by one vote over Scullin's deputy, Frank Forde. His first priority was to reunite the party; he set about strengthening the anti-Lang forces in New South Wales, a task made easier by the maverick Premier's dismissal by the state governor, Sir Philip Game. But the overriding threat was the likelihood of war, with the rise of fascism in Europe and, closer to home, a militaristic Japanese empire.

Curtin was more pessimistic – or perhaps prescient – than most. His family recalled a rare evening at home in the west, with Curtin and his daughter looking out at the Indian Ocean from Cottesloe Beach.

"Thinking of the election, Dad?" Elsie asked.

"No, not the election."

"Then what?"

"I was just thinking, what we would do, what our reactions would be, if we saw the Jap fleet coming in past the island now?"

"Do you think they ever will?"

"I've stopped wondering if they ever will," her father replied. "The only question to be answered now is when."

The Labor Party, with its mixed membership of isolationists, pacifists, international socialists, communists, Catholics and opportunists, was impossible to unite on the prospect of conflict. The Spanish Civil War alone nearly caused another split; Curtin, while declaring his sympathy for the republican government, was forced to take a position of studied neutrality. As a result of what was portrayed by its opponents as isolationism, and therefore lack of support for the Empire, the reunited Labor opposition gained only 2 seats at the 1937 election.

Until the actual declaration of war Curtin was seen as an appeaser. The impression was confirmed when he refused to join a government of national unity, as proposed by Prime Minister Robert Menzies and endorsed by many in his own caucus, especially the power-hungry Bert Evatt. Curtin's rationale was simple and logical: "If there could be anything worse than a government consisting of two parties it would be a government consisting of three parties. Such a combination would not be a government, it would be a society of disputation and debate; decisions could never be reached; determinations could not be arrived at, let alone carried out."

During 1940 he was under sustained attack within caucus from Evatt and others who resented his close co-operation with Menzies in the conduct of the war, and in the election that year he nearly lost his own seat. His political future seemed tenuous at best. But with the resignation of Menzies and the defection of the independents from the Fadden government power was thrust upon him anyway, and to the surprise of many he rose to it and embraced it.

His biographer Lloyd Ross saw the transformation: "From the day Curtin became Prime Minister his personality seemed to change. No longer neurotic nor lackadaisical he grew determined and ruthless in enforcing his basic ideas. His health improved and his serenity and confidence infected those who came into close contact with him."

It was just as well; a mere two months later the Japanese air force bombed Pearl Harbor and Curtin formally declared war on Japan – not as an appendage of Britain but as the independent nation of Australia. His rhetoric was Churchillian: he spoke to the men and women of Australia of "Australia's darkest hour" and "your inflexible determination that we as a nation of free people shall survive."

With the Japanese advancing through Malaya and no help from Britain in sight, in an article in the Melbourne *Herald* he penned the famous words: "Australia looks to America, free of any pangs as to our traditional links or kinship with the United Kingdom." Churchill was furious, but the Philippines were invaded; in New Guinea Rabaul and Ambon were taken; Singapore fell; and four days later Darwin was bombed. To most Australians it seemed that Curtin's decision was not only correct but inevitable.

The rift with Churchill deepened when Curtin demanded

the return of two Australian divisions which Churchill had designated for Burma. Churchill eventually acquiesced, but the troops had to return without escort, a trip of some fourteen days. Curtin, feeling personally responsible for their safety, barely slept for the fortnight. "How can I sleep while our transports are in the Indian Ocean with the Japanese submarines looking for them?" he said to Frank Green, Clerk of the House of Representatives, who found him pacing the lawns of the Lodge at midnight.

Towards the end of 1942 he had to make another deeply traumatic decision: he reversed his lifelong opposition to conscription for overseas service to allow Australian conscripts to fight in a limited area of the Pacific, specifically in New Guinea. His argument was essentially one of fairness: American conscripts under the command of General Douglas MacArthur, now based in Australia, were fighting far from home in Australia's defence. It was only just that Australians should do the same. With difficulty he shepherded the policy through the party's conference and caucus, but he was never totally comfortable with it.

On the whole Curtin and MacArthur got on well, but the tensions involved in having a foreigner effectively in charge of his country's military policy undoubtedly took their toll. He also faced a hostile conservative press, led by Keith Murdoch in Melbourne and Frank Packer in Sydney. He was able to circumvent them to some extent by ensuring good personal relations with the Canberra press gallery, most of whom he treated as friends and confidants. So close was the relationship that Curtin was able to brief what was known as his circus off the record, a trust that was never betrayed.

There is a story of one of Curtin's confrontations with a press baron – probably Murdoch – which illustrates the difference. When the proprietor sought to give him some directions, Curtin jibbed. "I'm afraid I had to talk very straight to him," said the Prime Minister, describing the interview later. "I said to this man: 'I want you to understand that I obey nobody else but the people of Australia. You may as well know now that you have nothing in the world that I want.'" His friend Victor Courtney regarded the exchange as his finest memory of John Curtin.

Certainly the press attacks did not dint his popularity. At the 1943 election Labor won 50 per cent of the primary vote, including 60 per cent of that of the troops. From then on Curtin could pursue his policies from a secure base. With MacArthur in effective control of the military counter-attacks, Curtin turned his mind to his true ambition: the transformation of post-war Australia into a democratic socialist state.

He had already set up a new Ministry of Post-War Reconstruction with the dynamic H.C. "Nugget" Coombs as director and a dedicated team who were to dominate the Australian public service for the next decade and beyond. He instituted a radical program of tax reform to distribute the country's wealth more equitably and introduced widows' pensions, maternity allowances, and funeral, unemployment and sickness benefits. And he adopted a Keynesian approach to economic planning, restoring the goal of full employment as the government's priority. He laid the groundwork for a massive increase in immigration and the development of a network of universities.

But there were limits to what was possible. The economy

remained on a war footing and Curtin's own austerity program meant that the government could not contemplate expansionary budgets. His attempts to expand Commonwealth power, first through a constitutional convention and then through a referendum, were thwarted by Menzies, who was determined to resist what he saw as the rising tide of socialism.

And he was only partly successful in mending fences with Britain in a trip to London for that purpose in 1944. Although Curtin declared himself determined to end what he called "the Tories' monopoly of the union jack", appointed the Duke of Gloucester rather than an Australian as Governor-General (his party had wanted Scullin, who was reluctant) and insisted that Australia was a country of "seven million Britishers", Churchill rejected his call for an Imperial Secretariat to take control of the war; the mother country was resolved to teach its fractious infant a lesson. With the withdrawal of its troops for home defence, Australia's principal role was to supply food and other materials to Britain, a demand Curtin loyally fulfilled.

He returned to Australia exhausted and in October suffered a severe heart attack, which hospitalised him for two months. In January 1945 he was back in his office, but his lifetime of smoking, long hours and poor diet, and his earlier alcohol abuse, were catching up with him. In April his lungs gave out, and on his final release from hospital he announced, "I'm not worth two bob." He died on July 5; the Japanese surrendered just forty days later.

His contemporaries knew John Curtin as a shy and somewhat aloof man with a taste for sport, books and musical comedy; his favourite songs were said to be "Sweet

Genevieve" and "Little Grey Home in the West". He called himself a simple, ordinary man. But in extraordinary times he achieved, if not greatness, something very close to it. His responsibilities made him a lonely figure, but one universally admired for his selflessness, dedication and courage. The inscription on his tombstone in Perth's Karrakatta Cemetery reads:

> His country was his pride
> His brother man his cause

FRANCIS MICHAEL **FORDE**

Frank Forde is generally remembered for just one thing: his name is the answer to the trivia question, "Who was Australia's shortest-serving Prime Minister?"

Forde was the stop-gap who held the post for just eight days between the death of John Curtin and the election of Ben Chifley. To achieve this moment of fame he spent some thirty-seven years in state and federal parliament, fourteen of them as deputy to three different Labor leaders. It was a long apprenticeship, but one which Forde accepted with commendable diligence and unswerving loyalty. His contemporaries considered him the ultimate team player, an ideal party man.

Francis Michael Forde was born in Mitchell, Queensland, in 1890. His Irish immigrant parents, noting his early intelligence and curiosity, scraped together enough money to send him to the Christian Brothers' school at Toowoomba, where he also trained as a teacher. His early jobs included working as a railway clerk and a telegraphist, as a result of which he joined the post office and was transferred to Rockhampton in 1914.

Like many Irish Australians he was drawn into the anti-conscription campaign and joined the ALP; when the pro-conscription state member for Rockhampton was expelled from the party, Forde won the seat in the ensuing by-election. He held it in 1918 and 1920, and then in 1922 William Higgs, the Labor member for the federal seat of Capricornia, was also expelled. Forde took his seat and arrived in Melbourne as the youngest member of the House of Representatives.

When Labor gained government in 1929, he was immediately promoted to the frontbench as Assistant Minister for Trade and Customs and next year assumed the portfolio in cabinet, where he fought for a protectionist, high-tariff policy in an attempt to shield Australia from the Great Depression. The effort was unsuccessful, but Forde survived the landslide defeat of 1931 and became James Scullin's deputy.

He was seen as the natural successor, but on Scullin's resignation a faction within the party started a push for the more talented John Curtin. Others had their doubts: Curtin was known as a heavy drinker and a man of somewhat erratic habits. Forde expected to win, but in the end was defeated by a single vote in the caucus of twenty-one.

He remained deputy, and on Labor's return to power in 1941 became Minister for War, a difficult portfolio in which he frequently clashed with Australia's top military commander, the opinionated General Thomas Blamey. He served as acting Prime Minister twice, when Curtin was overseas and when he was ill, and once again saw himself in line for the top job. But during Curtin's final illness Forde himself was out of the country as a delegate to the United Nations Conference on International Organization, where he was overshadowed by Bert Evatt.

Ben Chifley was acting Prime Minister until Forde's return three days before Curtin's death; on 5 July 1945 Forde was commissioned as Prime Minister, but at the caucus meeting a week later the popular Chifley, who had been Curtin's own choice as his successor, defeated him easily. It may have been some consolation to Forde that the vote choosing him as deputy over Evatt was almost unanimous.

His last two years in Canberra were hard ones; as Minister for Defence he was blamed for the slow demobilisation of the troops and back in Rockhampton he was accused of deserting his electorate, having moved his family to Sydney. In the 1946 election he lost the seat of Capricornia. But there was an upside: Chifley sent him to Ottawa as high commissioner to Canada, and in 1950 Robert Menzies renewed the appointment.

Forde described the period as the happiest of his life, but when he returned in 1954 he immediately returned to politics. He was preselected for the federal seat of Wide Bay, but was unsuccessful at the election; instead he won the outback seat of Flinders in the state parliament. But the Labor split ruined any chance of a comeback and he lost his seat in 1957. He failed to win it back in 1960 and was rejected for the Senate in 1962. At the age of seventy-two his active political career was finally over.

But he had become something of an institution, seldom rejecting an invitation to a function. Notably, Menzies sent him to represent Australia at the funeral of Douglas MacArthur, and Gough Whitlam invited him to his victory lunch in 1972. He remained vigorous until his death in 1983; he might have been the shortest serving Prime Minister, but at the time he was the longest-lived. His death had its own repercussions; after attending his state funeral the influential party member John Button cornered his leader Bill Hayden and persuaded him to stand down in favour of Bob Hawke, who led Labor back to power and became its longest serving Prime Minister.

And a final footnote: in 1992 Forde's daughter-in-law Leneen Forde was appointed as Queensland's first female governor. Frank Forde might have spent most of his career as a bridesmaid, but his life cannot be encapsulated in a single answer on trivia night.

JOSEPH BENEDICT CHIFLEY

IF JOHN CURTIN was probably Australia's most admired Prime Minister, Ben Chifley was almost certainly its best loved. The humble, plain-spoken engine driver from Bathurst had an affinity with ordinary men and women that has seldom been approached and never been bettered.

During the war years, as Treasurer, he was Curtin's stalwart and the human face of his government, and as peacetime Prime Minister he oversaw much of the ambitious program he and his predecessor had initiated. He was a shrewd and effective politician and unchallenged within his party. Yet he won only one election and after his defeat Labor spent twenty-three years in opposition. In hard political terms it was not an inspiring record, yet no one is ranked higher in the ALP's pantheon.

Joseph Benedict Chifley was born in 1885, the son of a native-born blacksmith and an Irish domestic servant. The family was devoutly Catholic and aggressively proud of its origins; much later Ben (as he was always known) was to boast: "I am the descendant of a race that fought a long and bitter fight against perjurers and pimps and liars."

His life was disrupted at the age of five when for reasons which are not clear he was separated from his brothers and sisters and sent to live on his grandparents' farm; he became a general labourer and slept on chaff bags on an earth floor in a wattle-and-daub hut. His education at the local bush school was basic and sporadic, but it gave him a taste for reading and a thirst for knowledge which were reinforced by his first-hand experience of the rural depression of the 1890s.

Before he returned to his parents' home and the Patrician Brothers' High School in 1899, his course was set. When his grandfather asked him what he wanted as his career, the boy replied without hesitation: "A member of parliament."

More immediately he held a succession of unskilled jobs before applying to join the NSW State Railways, while continuing his studies at night. Ten years later he was the state's youngest fully qualified engine driver, a job he enjoyed immensely. He was also an enthusiastic unionist. In 1914 he married Elizabeth McKenzie, who was, to his parents' horror, a zealous Presbyterian. The wedding took place in a Protestant church. "One of us has to take the knock," said Chifley. "It had better be me." His political skills were already evident.

During the war years he opposed conscription and led the Bathurst workers in a strike in 1917, which resulted in his dismissal. He was reinstated, but it was not until Jack Lang became Premier in 1925 that his full seniority was restored. By that time he was a dedicated party member himself; he had failed to gain preselection for the state seat of Bathurst, but in 1925 he stood unsuccessfully for the federal seat of Macquarie. He won the seat in 1928.

His first speeches in parliament centred on industrial relations, but they soon broadened into a discussion of the economy as a whole, a subject on which the largely self-educated engine driver proved remarkably erudite. He was not immediately included in James Scullin's ministry, but as the Depression hit and the party split in 1931 he was given the then junior portfolio of Defence. He could have gone further: Joe Lyons offered him the Treasury if he would join his faction and cross to the UAP, but Chifley stayed loyal.

He lost his seat in the landslide of 1931 and devoted himself to opposing the Langites in his home state; he became president of the ALP's official NSW branch. In 1934 he actually stood against Lang in the former Premier's own stronghold of Auburn; predictably he lost and permanently damaged his vocal cords in the process. He had once been described as "the silver-tongued orator from the west"; reminded of this he quipped: "There's no silver there now, boy, just a lot of rusty old chains knocking together."

He had also failed to regain Macquarie in 1934; however, in 1935 Lyons invited him to represent Labor on the Royal Commission into Banking and Finance. It was a great learning experience and led him to a commitment to the nationalisation of banking. He was subsequently appointed director of labour supply and regulation in the Ministry of Munitions, a position from which he formed a close working relationship with the industrialist Essington Lewis.

In 1940 he finally won back Macquarie and joined Curtin in advocating moderation in the hung parliament that followed. When Labor took over in 1941, he was the obvious choice for Curtin's Treasurer, a role in which he took much of the domestic burden for his close friend. Chifley's popularity on both sides of parliament also made him the ideal candidate for the difficult job of running government business in parliament; he was the first leader of the house in the modern sense. And he was Curtin's principal link to the factionalised Labor caucus and the wider party organisation.

He still found time to introduce some major economic reforms, including uniform taxation and the pay-as-you-earn system. As part of his comprehensive plan to finance the war effort he pegged wages and profits and raised taxation overall. His political skills made such drastic moves not only acceptable, but even popular with a patriotic electorate. Many still regard him as Australia's most successful Treasurer. And in 1942 he took a second ministry: Post-War Reconstruction. He staffed it mainly with bright young men and women from outside the public service, but at its head was the formidable public banker H.C. "Nugget" Coombs. Coombs and Chifley were to develop a mutual respect and friendship that lasted until Chifley's death. Between them, they determined much of Australia's agenda for the decade that followed and beyond.

Certainly, Coombs became Chifley's most important adviser from 1945, when Curtin died in office and Chifley easily won the caucus ballot that followed. As Prime Minister he had a formidable workload, but he decided to retain the Treasury as well, to the consternation of some of his colleagues. He was considered a fit man, keen on walking and sport, and although his trademark pipe was seldom out of his mouth, it was only occasionally lit. To Dame Enid Lyons he appeared like "a Great Dane, with his rugged good looks, his immense personal dignity and his friendly, but always slightly reserved, bearing".

And he retained the common touch. He refused to purchase or wear a dinner suit, even to meet King George VI on an official visit to London. He preferred to travel by train or, when that was not possible, by car; on his regular commutes from Bathurst to Canberra he liked to stop for a steak at a café in Gundagai. On one occasion the proprietor apologised that due to war shortages he was unable to find the onions that the Prime Minister liked as garnish. "We can fix that," replied Chifley, pulling a couple of succulent bulbs from his coat pocket.

Famously, Chifley refused to move into the Lodge, electing to remain at the more humble Hotel Kurrajong. But as was often the case with Chifley, the reasons for this were more complex than they seemed. After an early miscarriage, his wife Elizabeth had become barren and relapsed into a semi-invalid state; she was more or less housebound, coming to Canberra rarely and only for ceremonial occasions. Chifley remained a devoted husband, but he had also embarked on a longstanding affair with his secretary, Phyllis Donnelly; he may also have had a brief liaison with her elder sister Nell. It was easier to be discreet about the arrangement at the Kurrajong than it would have been in the Prime Minister's official residence. But that said, there is no reason to doubt that the frugal Chifley regarded the Lodge as an unnecessary extravagance at a time of national economic restraint.

In keeping with his man-of-the-people image, Chifley's first overseas trip was to visit the troops awaiting discharge in Papua New Guinea. Subsequently he visited New Zealand, the United Kingdom and the United States, where he showed his bargaining skill with the then Under-Secretary of State, Dean Acheson. After official talks over the repayment of the

Lend Lease agreement had stalled, Coombs reported that Chifley picked up the phone and asked to speak to Dean Acheson and a conversation on these lines followed:

Chifley: Mr Secretary, you know our officials have been talking about the Lend Lease settlement. They tell me there is a difference between us about the amount that is due to you. You make it $US32 million and we make it $US22 million. I know this is a matter of high policy and I wouldn't want you to think I am bargaining but I have to leave for Japan and I wonder whether we couldn't do a quick deal and settle it.

Acheson: What sort of a deal have you in mind?

Chifley: Suppose we split the difference and call it $US27 million in complete and final settlement.

Acheson (after a short pause): Done, Mr Prime Minister.

Chifley: It's a deal.

Not all negotiations were so simple. In 1946 Chifley had the task of selling his party the Bretton Woods Agreement. Chifley was personally in favour of establishing the International Monetary Fund and the World Bank, but the Labor movement had a long and understandable hostility towards international financiers, whom it saw as the "Mr Moneybags" types who had done so much damage during the Great Depression and played a major part in bringing down the Scullin government. He manoeuvred acceptance through the party's federal executive, but his caucus demanded a special federal conference on the issue. So Chifley went back to the states and persuaded three state executives to oppose holding such a conference, and then returned to caucus with a promise of lower taxes and a rise in pensions. In the ensuing euphoria Bretton Woods sneaked through.

While his integrity was undisputed, he was always the pragmatist. "You have to be scrupulously honest," he once advised a new member, "but there's nothing to stop you being a bit bloody foxy." This practical side also came out during a visit to India, where Prime Minister Jawaharlal Nehru was lamenting the loneliness of power.

"I suppose it would be valuable to have someone who would support you when you were right," Nehru mused.

Chifley rejoined: "Even more valuable if you happened to be wrong."

Chifley was never the radical socialist that Curtin was; even when he moderated his views in later life, Curtin never lost his Utopian streak. His successor was more interested in steady reform than radical change, but social justice was always the priority. Hence the basis of all Chifley's policies was full employment. He was especially concerned that the returning troops should be treated better than their World War I fathers had been, and introduced not only job preferences for soldiers, but scholarships, training schemes and a universal gratuity. He also set up the Commonwealth Employment Service.

After winning the 1946 election, albeit with a reduced majority, he initiated the great post-war immigration program, started up the motor vehicle industry, subsidised the state hospital system to provide free public wards, appointed a second Australian-born Governor-General in the former NSW Premier Bill McKell and inaugurated an independent news service for the Australian Broadcasting Corporation to compete with the anti-Labor private media. This last infuriated the press barons, but they were never on side anyway. And he showed his caution when he refused to involve the

Commonwealth in the state responsibility of school funding; he was well aware of the potential for sectarian division. Reminded that the Commonwealth was already involved in pre-school and university education, Chifley replied: "That's different – they're for kids before they've got souls and after they've lost them."

But then came the crunch: after what had been thought to be a routine cabinet meeting Chifley's press secretary Don Rodgers issued a 42-word release to the assembled reporters: "Cabinet today authorised the Attorney-General (Dr Evatt) and myself to prepare legislation for submission to the federal parliamentary Labor Party for the nationalisation of banking, other than state banks, with proper protection for the shareholders, depositors, borrowers and staffs of private banks." It is reported that one usually phlegmatic pressman was so astounded that he bit through the stem of his pipe. Chifley had hoped that less draconian legislation, which the parliament had passed in 1945, would bring the banks to heel. But a challenge to one aspect of it in the High Court had already succeeded and it was obvious that others would follow. With some personal reluctance, Chifley decided that full nationalisation was the only answer, although he was well aware of both the legal and political dangers inherent in the decision.

It was a gamble from which Chifley never recovered. The banks and their supporters spared no effort in the campaign that followed. Chifley's protégé Fred Daly recalled a meeting clearly stacked with bank employees. He accused one of them: "You're a bank officer and you're being paid time and a half to come here and interject." The man replied: "That's a deliberate lie, I get double time." In the event the High

Court ruled that the legislation was unconstitutional, but the damage was done.

The party's own troops were demoralised and also confused; when the coal miners in the Hunter district went on strike Chifley introduced draconian legislation to jail the strike leaders and broke the strike by sending in the armed forces. This was contrary to both the letter and spirit of Labor policy, but Chifley justified his actions on the grounds that the strike had been engineered by the communists, the enemies of the ALP. No other leader could have got away with it, but Chifley's hold over the caucus and the wider movement was such that he was actually applauded for his resolution. However, Labor was routed at the 1949 election, with the resurgent Robert Menzies's promise to end petrol rationing another potent factor.

Chifley's own campaign performance was curiously lacklustre, with the exception of what is his most remembered speech: "It is the duty and responsibility of the community, and particularly those more fortunately placed, to see that our less fortunate citizens are protected from those shafts of fate that leave them helpless and without hope … that is the objective for which we are striving. It is the beacon, the light on the hill, to which our eyes are always turned and to which our efforts are always directed." It is often forgotten that those words were uttered in the context not of victory, but of imminent defeat.

The defeat was all the more devastating because it was unexpected: Chifley and Labor believed that their achievements in getting Australia through the war and its aftermath had made Labor the natural party of government, with Menzies's refurbished Liberals confined to the fringe. Labor still controlled the Senate and could block conservative legislation, but Menzies, exploiting well-nourished fears of communism and the growing rifts within Labor, ended that with the double dissolution of 1951.

Again, Chifley seemed unwilling to throw himself into the fight. He was not suited to opposition; his colleagues said there was not enough hate in him. And his health was failing after a heart attack in 1950. Evatt's driving ambition for the leadership was also taking a toll. Chifley became something of a recluse, spending much of his time consuming tea and toast in his room at the Kurrajong. He was there with Phyllis Donnelly on the night of 13 June 1951, while his colleagues were celebrating Australia's golden jubilee at a banquet and ball at Parliament House. At the height of the festivities Don Rodgers arrived to inform the guests that Chifley had died from a massive heart attack.

When the interior minister in charge of the function, Sir Wilfrid Kent-Hughes, kept the band playing, Fred Daly went straight to Menzies and demanded that the music be stopped. Menzies immediately concurred and the celebration became a wake. Both Menzies and Evatt wept unashamedly. It says much for the esteem and affection in which Chifley was held that his death could reduce two such hardened politicians to tears.

HAROLD EDWARD HOLT

NO AUSTRALIAN PRIME Minister ever came to the job better prepared than Harold Holt.

He entered parliament in 1935 as a protégé of Robert Menzies and succeeded his patron and mentor thirty-one years later. In the interim he held a number of senior portfolios, notably Labour and National Service, Immigration and Treasury, and was deputy leader of his party for a decade.

And the times were propitious. In 1966 the conservatives were in power in four of the six states and held a comfortable majority in Canberra, and with the DLP holding the balance of power in the Senate were in effective control of both houses. Labor was led by Arthur Calwell, a formidable politician in his prime but now well past it and a two-time loser; with nearly a year to consolidate before the election was due, Holt had every reason to anticipate an easy transition into power and a continuation of the seventeen years of uninterrupted conservative rule. As it turned out, his regime was not to be a new beginning, but the beginning of the end.

Harold Edward Holt was born in Sydney in 1908; his father, Tom, was a schoolteacher, but had a yen for a more Bohemian life. He briefly tried the hotel trade in Adelaide but soon went on the road as a theatrical manager. The young Harold began his education at Randwick Public School before being sent to board at Abbotsholme in Killara, where he met the young Billy McMahon; but at the age of eleven he was transferred to Wesley College in Melbourne, the alma mater of Robert Menzies.

His main pursuits were sport and theatrical activities – he had inherited his father's fascination with show business, as did his brother Cliff, who was a manager with the Hoyts chain, and he had an aunt who performed in musical comedies. But even so he did well enough to win a scholarship to Melbourne University, from which, after winning a prize for oratory, he graduated in law in 1930. The Depression ruled out a career at the bar; Holt set up as a solicitor but increasingly found himself involved in theatrical circles.

His father was now in partnership with the entrepreneur Frank Thring, father of the actor; Harold took out Thring's daughter for a while, only to have his father sweep her off her feet and marry her. Deeply hurt, he sought refuge in politics.

Mingling effortlessly in Melbourne's social milieu, the dashing and charming Holt had come to the attention of Menzies and another powerful figure, Dame Mabel Brookes; they inducted him into the Young Nationalists, and in 1934 Holt stood quixotically for the UAP in the seat of Yarra against Jim Scullin. He contested a state Labor seat and lost again, but in 1935 the safe federal seat of Fawkner became vacant; Holt won it easily in a by-election and entered parliament at the age of twenty-seven.

When Menzies took over the leadership of the UAP in 1939, he gave Holt a couple of junior positions, but had to sack him from them in 1940 when the Country Party returned to the coalition and demanded the jobs for its own members. Holt went off to join the Australian Imperial Force; it might have been the end of his career, but before he had resigned from parliament a tragic air accident killed three senior ministers. Menzies secured Holt's release from the armed forces and immediately promoted him to the important Ministry of Labour and National Service, where he introduced child endowment and acquired the title "Godfather to a million children".

But the following year he was drawn into the push to oust Menzies, and although he remained in Arthur Fadden's ministry, in 1941 he followed his leader into opposition, where he spent the next eight years, albeit on the frontbench. He was still seen as a man with a future; one of her party's arbiters, Dame Enid Lyons, wrote of him: "Harold Holt at 35 was the baby of the party. A young bachelor, fond of social life and an ardent racegoer, he had gained a reputation as a playboy. I expected not to like him but from the beginning I saw in him qualities that suggested far greater depths of character than appeared on the glossy surface."

The playboy image was somewhat mitigated when in 1946 he married Zara Dickins, whom he had met at university. The two had planned to wed, but Holt decided he could not support a family on what was then a meagre solicitor's income. On the rebound, Zara married a British Army officer. However, she kept in touch with Holt; indeed, he fathered at least two and possibly all three of her sons. Finally the marriage failed and the two were formally reunited.

Menzies led the conservatives back to power in 1949 and immediately re-appointed his protégé to Labour and National Service, and then threw in Immigration as well. Holt thrived on the work; he travelled a lot and he and Zara maintained a vigorous social life; he never really ceased to be the playboy that Dame Enid had identified.

This told against him in 1956 when Sir Eric Harrison resigned from parliament, leaving the position of deputy leader open; Holt, with Menzies's support, was expected to win easily but in fact scraped in by a single vote. It was enough. He was now clearly the heir apparent and when Arthur Fadden retired in 1958, Holt reclaimed the Treasury for his party. As he had in the Ministry of Labour and National Service, he relied heavily on his departmental officers and blamed them when an ill-advised credit squeeze nearly cost the coalition government at the 1961 election. It regained the lost ground in 1963, and when Holt brought down his last budget in 1965, Menzies walked over to him and ruffled his hair in a fatherly fashion – an official anointment which caused Holt both pleasure and embarrassment.

But it was all pleasure when he was elected leader unopposed in 1966: he had done it, he boasted to Zara, without stepping over a single dead body. Perhaps this was the problem; because it had all come so easily, Holt lacked the necessary toughness to keep his troops in line. Menzies had been, quite simply, unchallengeable: "the great white chief", as Holt called him, had ruled the party by personal fiat. Under the more relaxed Holt, backbenchers in particular began to get restive.

The first year was alright; in parliament Holt had the ageing Calwell's measure and although dissent against

Australia's involvement in Vietnam was starting to be heard, there was no cause for alarm. Holt made a ceremonial visit to Washington, where he assured President Lyndon Johnson that Australia was "all the way with LBJ", an affirmation of loyalty which some critics found unnecessarily servile. But the two men formed a genuine friendship and when Johnson made a return visit a month before the 1966 election, it led to the government's return with a record majority.

In his first year Holt had cautiously begun to unwind the White Australia policy, although in practice it was not really abolished until Gough Whitlam came to power in 1972. In his second year he ran a referendum to have Aboriginal Australians counted in the census and to allow the Commonwealth, as well as the states, to make laws on their behalf. It was passed with a huge majority and is now counted as one of Holt's triumphs, although in fact, as with the White Australia policy, Holt went on to ensure that it had no immediate effect.

In its second year the government began to struggle. A revolt by backbenchers forced Holt to hold a second royal commission into the sinking of HMAS *Voyager*; then there was a scandal over the use of VIP aircraft which Holt and his Minister for Air, Peter Howson, gravely mishandled. But worst of all was the fact that Whitlam had finally succeeded Calwell as Labor leader and established his ascendancy over Holt in parliament. Holt complained to colleagues that it wasn't fair; whenever he was getting on top of the argument, Whitlam changed the subject.

This only reinforced the doubts many were starting to harbour and the half-Senate election later in the year reinforced them; the coalition primary vote shrank to 43 per cent compared with Labor's 45. By the time parliament adjourned for the year, there was a sizeable bloc conspiring against his leadership.

Circumstances forestalled them. On December 27 Holt led a group of friends, including his mistress at the time, Marjorie Gillespie, to the lonely Cheviot Beach on the bleak Nepean Peninsula. They had been partying enthusiastically through the festive season at the social hub of Portsea and were in a reckless mood. Holt unwisely decided to take an early morning swim; he plunged into the wild surf and was never seen again. There were silly stories that he had been picked up by a Chinese submarine and cruel ones that he was suicidal as a result of his inability to handle his job, but the truth is almost certainly simpler: he was showing off in front of his girlfriend.

His death was the occasion of a grand memorial service in Melbourne, attended by Prince Charles, the British Prime Minister Harold Wilson, numerous regional dignitaries and, of course, Johnson, who paid moving tribute to his friend. The Americans renamed their defence facility at North West Cape the Harold E. Holt station. Rather more prosaically, and perhaps less tastefully, the Malvern Council in Melbourne renamed their swimming pool after the drowned Prime Minister.

JOHN McEWEN

BLACK JACK MCEWEN was, like his Country Party predecessors, only a stop-gap Prime Minister; he held the job for just twenty-three days.

But his political footprint remains a bigger one than some of those who lasted much longer. More than any other single person McEwen transformed Australia's post-war trade structure, and with it the economy and foreign policy. Both physically and politically he was a formidable presence.

John McEwen was born in Chiltern, Victoria, in 1900, the son of Irish immigrants. His mother died when he was two and his father when he was seven, and the boy was sent to live with his grandmother Nellie Porter, first at Wangaratta and later at Dandenong. Mrs Porter gave him an early piece of advice: never settle for second best. "If you go into the church, become an archbishop. If you go into the army, become a general. If you go into politics, become Prime Minister." So he did.

But in the meantime he was forced to leave school at the

age of thirteen, and after a series of odd jobs took the Commonwealth public service exam. He was placed in the crown solicitor's office under Fred Whitlam, the father of Gough. But when he turned eighteen he resigned to join the army and volunteered for overseas service in World War I. He was still in camp when peace came, but was eligible for a soldier-settler's grant, despite having no background in farming.

He convinced the authorities to give him thirty-eight hectares of untilled land near Stanhope, Victoria, and for the next few years lived in a shanty on a staple diet of wild rabbits. His only reading was a dictionary, which he devoured from cover to cover, giving himself an extensive vocabulary which was to become a constant surprise to his urban colleagues. His loneliness was relieved in 1921 when he married Annie McLeod; she proved a willing and capable helpmate in developing both the farm and McEwen's burgeoning political career.

To secure capital to equip his farm, he spent some time as a wharfie in Melbourne, working under another man's name, and in spite of the collapse of dairy prices built up his holding to over 1200 hectares and was able to survive the Depression. But most of his neighbours did not, and their despair as they were forced to walk off their land affected him deeply. While still a teenager he had been active in the Victorian Farmers Union, one of the sponsors of the Country Party, which he joined on its formation in 1926.

A few years later he led a deputation of soldier-settlers to confront the state Attorney-General, Robert Menzies. Many years afterwards Menzies still remembered the encounter: "You know, you were terrifying even when you were quite young," he said to McEwen. It was Menzies who christened him "Black Jack", a nickname which stuck all his life.

These experiences drove McEwen to seek political office. In 1932 he stood unsuccessfully for state parliament and then secured preselection for the federal seat of Echuca (later renamed Indi and then Murray), which he won in 1934. From 1937 to 1939 he was Joe Lyons's Minister for the Interior and when the Country Party rejoined the coalition in 1940 he became Minister for External Affairs and then Minister for Air and Civil Aviation, a post he retained under Fadden.

McEwen himself had made a bid for the party leadership in 1939 and again in 1940, but when he and Earle Page were deadlocked on a tied vote, Fadden was appointed as a compromise. McEwen became Fadden's deputy in 1943. Thus when the coalition was returned in 1949, Fadden got the Treasury and McEwen the Ministry of Commerce and Agriculture, later to become Trade. But over the years, with the help of his departmental heads John Crawford and Alan Westerman, he turned the relatively junior ministry into a power base able to challenge Treasury on its own ground.

These were his glory years: almost single-handedly he took Australia from being a supplier of raw materials to Britain to a world trader with diverse markets and a diverse output. In 1957, just twelve years after the end of the war, he signed a trade agreement with Japan. With memories of Changi and the Burma railway still fresh in Australian minds it was an audacious and not always popular move, but McEwen saw it as an opportunity too profitable to ignore.

He became a champion not only of primary producers but also of local secondary industry. His reasoning was that manufacturing was the major employer, so to prevent unemployment it must be protected by tariffs. And if this raised the price of goods for rural workers, then they must be subsidised in return.

This policy of all-round protectionism was bitterly opposed by Treasury and by its ministers, first Harold Holt and later Billy McMahon, but McEwen usually had Menzies's backing and won more times than he lost. His only serious defeat came at the hands of Holt, who in 1967 stood him up on the question of devaluing the currency.

This was just before Holt's death, the occasion of McEwen's brief prime ministership and most controversial political act. When the news broke, McEwen went straight to the Governor-General, Lord Casey, expecting to be commissioned immediately. There was, after all, a precedent: when Lyons died in office, Page succeeded him. But, Casey pointed out, in 1939 the senior UAP did not have a deputy; in 1967 the Liberals had Billy McMahon. McEwen replied flatly that neither he nor his party would serve under McMahon, with whom he had had a long and bitter relationship.

Casey temporised, and talked to a number of senior Liberals, but eventually acquiesced; McEwen would become Prime Minister but only until the Liberals elected a new leader. Even then there were some who recalled the Fadden precedent of 1941 and wanted McEwen to stay on, at least until the next election. But this would have been seen as an admission that the Liberal Party had no one worthy of becoming head of state. McMahon, still hoping for the job, asked McEwen why he had been vetoed. McEwen replied bluntly: "Because I don't trust you."

He continued as deputy under John Gorton and more than once saved Gorton from his impetuosity, but eventually decided the man was incorrigible and in October 1970 formally withdrew his veto against McMahon. Four months later he retired from parliament and three months after that McMahon was Prime Minister.

At the break-up of parliament in 1972 the Country Party held a farewell function for its retiring members, which McMahon attended. He made a little speech, during which he said that during the previous week he had had a problem and his wife Sonia had suggested that he ring Jack McEwen about it. And, said McMahon, that was very, very good advice because McEwen had always been very, very helpful.

At which point a deep voice growled from the back of the room: "I'm still waiting for that phone call, Billy." Even in retirement, Black Jack was formidable. He died in 1980.

JOHN GREY **GORTON**

JOHN GORTON WAS the first of our prime ministers to become an abstract noun. No one ever talked of Deakinism or Scullinism, let alone Menziesism; but Gortonism became a mantra the conservatives used to frighten potential rebels back into line.

It meant creeping centralism, almost socialism, even a form of iconoclasm which defied Liberal shibboleths and conventions. It was a terrible shock to the establishment and the most shocking thing about it was that it nearly worked. John Grey Gorton might have been an accidental Prime Minister, but he was, for a period, a formidable one. His Labor opponents regarded him as a very near miss.

John Grey Gorton was born in 1911 in Melbourne and was illegitimate, a fact that only emerged late in his political life and confirmed his enemies' view that he really was a bastard. His father, John, was separated but not divorced from his wife, Kathleen, and had a de facto relationship with a woman named Alice Sinn. The pair had a son and a daughter, Ruth. But Alice died in 1918 and the family moved to Sydney, where Kathleen was prevailed upon to care for the children while their father moved back to Victoria to manage rural properties.

It was hardly a stable upbringing, but young John received the best of schooling, first as a boarder at Shore in Sydney, where he reportedly shared a dormitory with Errol Flynn, and then, when he moved south to rejoin his father, at Geelong Grammar. He was a popular student and a keen sportsman, but no great scholar; nonetheless when he left school in 1930, his father was persuaded to send him to Oxford, from which he returned with a master's degree, a pilot's licence and an American wife, Bettina.

He had hoped to join the Department of External Affairs, but was knocked back; he was on the verge of starting work as a journalist with the Melbourne *Herald* when his father died and he had to go home to run the family property at Lake Kangaroo. This consisted of a draughty house and an unprofitable orange orchard; Gorton had a rough four years, but they introduced him to politics. He joined the Country Party and became secretary of its Mystic Park branch.

The outbreak of war changed his life. He joined the Royal Australian Air Force and was posted to England; then, on the way to the Middle East, he was diverted to the defence of Singapore, where he crashed in action. He escaped the fall of the island on a ship which was torpedoed; he was rescued and ended up in Fremantle, from where, after plastic surgery, he was posted to Papua New Guinea. He saw further action and was involved in two more crashes. He ended the war as a flying instructor.

He returned to Australia as a glamorous ex-serviceman and promptly resumed his political career, but, like many other Victorians at the time, he deserted the Country Party to join the newly formed Liberals. He was elected to Kerang Shire Council and became mayor. He failed in a bid for the state Legislative Council, but won preselection for the Senate and was elected in the landslide of 1949.

Gorton arrived in Canberra as a convinced anti-socialist, but without any real program; from the first his determined independence of thought and action disturbed some of his Liberal colleagues. Menzies called him a mischief-maker and left him on the backbench for nine years. But he soon emerged as one of the best performers in a generally undistinguished chamber and eventually was appointed to a succession of junior ministries – navy, interior and public works. He had to wait for Menzies to retire before joining the cabinet as Minister for Education and Science and deputy leader of the Senate.

In 1967 he succeeded Denham Henty as the government's Senate leader and distinguished himself by saving the government from an embarrassing scandal involving the use of VIP aircraft. The responsible minister, Peter Howson, had insisted that passenger lists had been destroyed and Prime Minister Harold Holt had accepted his assurance; this was known to be untrue, and the situation was getting ugly before Gorton nonchalantly produced the missing documents in the Senate. His colleagues were greatly impressed and even before Holt's death some, including Malcolm Fraser, were talking of him as leadership material.

The moment came at the beginning of 1968. With Billy McMahon vetoed by the Country Party and Alan Fairhall –

who had just about had enough of politics – declaring himself a non-starter, Gorton's only serious rival was Paul Hasluck, who refused to campaign, believing the position should be his by right. Gorton and his backers, on the other hand, rounded up the young backbenchers, who saw the more voter-friendly Victorian as an effective counter to the rising Gough Whitlam, especially on television.

Together with a majority of his Senate colleagues they gave Gorton the numbers and he quickly consolidated his position. Hasluck was shunted off to Yarralumla as Governor-General and Fairhall soon eased himself into retirement. Only McMahon remained to rock the boat and he was held in check by the Country Party and Jack McEwen, with whom Gorton formed a close relationship; the two had much in common, including a dedication to what the drier Liberals (and the Treasury) derided as rural socialism.

Gorton was determined to do things his way. While Holt had seen himself in the role of chairman, Gorton was an unapologetic leader. He removed the longstanding head of the Prime Minister's Department, Sir John Bunting, and replaced him with the head of education, his friend and ally Lennox Hewitt; the public service was very miffed. And he appointed as his personal chief of staff a competent but very young and attractive woman, Ainsley Gotto. Eyebrows were raised, but at that stage Gorton's popularity was such that his colleagues were prepared to give him a go.

A group of young ministers, including Tom Hughes, Jim Killen, Andrew Peacock and Don Chipp, together with some sympathetic backbenchers, started a dinner group they called the Mushroom Club, because, they claimed, they were kept in the dark and fed on bullshit. Gorton heard about it and insisted on joining; he was given the ceremonial title Chief Spore.

It was not all fun and games: Gorton set up the first federal Ministry for Aboriginal Affairs and initiated major reforms in the social welfare system. He also started to move Australia to a more independent foreign policy, with no more Australian troops for Vietnam and a tougher attitude towards foreign investment. These latter announcements alarmed the Democratic Labor Party, on whose support the coalition government depended; Gorton had wanted to go to an early election in 1968, but the DLP blocked it. The delay was to prove all but fatal.

By the end of the year Gorton was in serious trouble. His policies were not a worry for the voters, but his private life was getting something of an airing; his indiscretions, as they were seen to be, had even been raised in parliament. Actually, they were pretty mild: Gorton had paid a lengthy visit to the dressing room of nightclub singer Liza Minnelli, had escorted a young female journalist to the American embassy for drinks after the press gallery's annual dinner, and there were constant snide remarks about his relationship with Ainsley Gotto. Well, so what? Chifley and McEwen had both conducted lengthy affairs with their secretaries, Holt's philandering was notorious, and even Menzies was said to have had a liaison with Dame Elizabeth Fairfax, wife of the press baron.

But they had all been reasonably discreet about their peccadilloes; Gorton seemed determined to flaunt his. The problem was encapsulated in an exchange with the DLP senator Vince Gair as Gorton was preparing to leave for a visit to Washington.

"Good luck," said Gair, "behave yourself."

Gorton took immediate offence: "John Grey Gorton will bloody well behave precisely as John Grey Gorton bloody well decides he wants to behave," he snapped back.

Gair, whose own behaviour was seldom exemplary, took the high ground: "Personally, I couldn't care if John Grey Gorton jumps into the Yarra and drowns himself," he proclaimed. "But John Grey Gorton also happens to be Prime Minister of Australia. I do care how John Grey Gorton conducts himself as Prime Minister of Australia."

So, it appeared, did some others. One Liberal member, Edward St John, was so offended that he actually resigned from the party and ran a sanctimonious crusade against Gorton until losing his seat at the 1969 election. But most ordinary people found the whole thing a bit of a joke; when unionists demonstrated in Sydney against the jailing of one of their number under federal legislation, one of the banners read: "Cut off Gorton's Penal Power." And in the media, satirists and cartoonists joined in. Gorton was given the nickname Jolly John.

While the public feeling towards him was still largely favourable, inside the party doubts were starting to emerge about whether he was serious enough for the job. It wasn't just the womanising. He was also a chain smoker and a heavy drinker, prone to taking the odd day off from parliament. His office used to excuse these by saying he had a touch of the flu; "Gorton flu" quickly became a euphemism for pissed as a parrot.

As the 1969 election approached, Gough Whitlam exploited the scuttlebutt mercilessly. When Gorton attacked his promise of a public health scheme as socialisation,

Whitlam replied: "I'm rather disappointed in the Prime Minister. Before this campaign we had a distinct understanding – that he wouldn't tell any lies about me if I didn't tell the truth about him." And he delighted in quoting Gorton's convoluted explanation of his own plans for health reform: "On the other hand the AMA agrees with us, or I believe, will agree with us, that it is its policy and it will be its policy to inform patients who ask what the common fee is and what our own fee is so that the patient will know whether he is going to be operated on, if that's what it is, on the basis of the common fee or not."

In the event there was a massive swing of nearly 7 per cent against the government; in one hit Holt's record majority was reduced to just 7 seats. The reaction in the Liberal Party was immediate and brutal: they decided that Gorton was a lost cause. McEwen appeared to concur; he publicly withdrew his veto of McMahon, who promptly challenged for the leadership. Gorton saw him off comfortably, but Whitlam was now clearly ascendant both in parliament and among the voters, and Gorton continued to make enemies.

To protect the Great Barrier Reef from oil drilling he asserted Commonwealth sovereignty over Australia's coastal waters, a direct attack on the Liberal sacred cow of states' rights. The premiers, led by the Liberal warlords Henry Bolte in Victoria and Robert Askin in New South Wales, made common cause against him. And the traditionalists in his own party room were outraged; only the intervention of McEwen prevented them from crossing the floor and bringing down the government.

His enemies were now remorseless, and when the party's vote failed to improve in the 1970 half-Senate election it was only a matter of time before they brought him down. In the end the trigger was pulled by one of Gorton's original backers, Malcolm Fraser. A messy row had developed between Fraser, the Defence Minister, and Andrew Peacock, the Army Minister. Gorton intervened on Peacock's behalf and both sides attempted to use the media by giving off-the-record briefings which only made things worse. With a censure motion from Labor looming, Fraser resigned from cabinet, accusing Gorton of damaging the party through a manic determination to get his own way. When Gorton put his own case, the journalist Alan Ramsey shouted from the press gallery: "You liar!"

At the party meeting next day, with the vote evenly split on a motion of confidence, Gorton resigned. Technically, he could probably have held on, but to do so would have precipitated a parliamentary vote of no confidence which, with his Liberal enemies prepared to cross the floor, would have brought down the government. This he was not prepared to do. And then, in an amazing turn-around, the party elected him as deputy leader to McMahon; this untenable situation prevailed for five months before Gorton wrote a series of newspaper articles giving his side of the argument and McMahon demanded, and received, his resignation from that post as well.

But he remained in parliament and returned to the frontbench as Bill Snedden's shadow Environment Minister. In opposition he co-sponsored a successful motion for the legalisation of homosexuality and campaigned for the legal use of both marijuana and heroin. He also became a vocal supporter of the arts in Australia. This surprised many of those who had thought him to be both a larrikin and a philistine, a public image he had cultivated while in office. But while he unashamedly liked gangster movies with lots of mayhem and big-breasted blondes, he was a cultivated man who wrote poetry in his spare time, some of which appeared pseudonymously in the *Canberra Times*. And he counted among his most important achievements his foundation of the Film and Television School and the Council for the Arts. One of his closest advisers in the area was the seemingly immortal "Nugget" Coombs.

Gorton resigned from the frontbench when Malcolm Fraser ousted Snedden as leader, and from the Liberal Party shortly afterwards. At the 1975 election he resigned his seat of Higgins to stand unsuccessfully as an independent senator. He then retired from formal politics, but remained an active and welcome figure at public functions for his favourite causes, one of which was attacking the Fraser government. In 1999 the Liberal Party re-admitted him to its ranks at a gala dinner, and he made a last public appearance at a banquet for his ninetieth birthday, attended by numerous friends and colleagues from both sides of politics. He died the following year and received the customary state funeral. But the eulogy was far from customary: Tom Hughes used it to launch a final devastating attack on Malcolm Fraser, who was also present and listened stony-faced. He must have thought that at last he was rid of his old adversary. But even in the grave, John Grey Gorton did things his way.

WILLIAM McMAHON

BILLY McMAHON CAME to the Lodge too late, in every sense. He was well past his political prime at sixty-three, older than any of his predecessors except John McEwen, who at sixty-seven was only ever seen as a stop-gap.

More importantly, after nearly twenty-two years the conservative era was finally drawing to a close. Menzies had left an impressive dynasty, but the best of them – Hasluck, Fairhall, Holt and Gorton – were now, for one reason or another, part of history. McMahon was literally the last man standing. And it showed. Holt had liked to describe himself as "first among equals"; the commentators were quick to label McMahon "worst among sequels".

His colleagues were not much kinder: within cabinet he had been known for some years as "Billy the Leak" because of his habit of passing secrets on to his media contacts, particularly employees of Consolidated Press, whose proprietor, Sir Frank Packer, openly referred to McMahon as "our man". Hasluck's diaries described him as "that treacherous little bastard McMahon". But even his worst enemies could not deny his ambition, indeed lust, for the job he finally gained on 10 March 1971.

William McMahon was born in 1908, to a well-off Sydney family, but both his parents died when he was young. He was brought up by his mother's relatives, principally by the Liberal MLC and lord mayor of Sydney Samuel Walder. He attended the Sydney Grammar School and went to St Paul's College at Sydney University to study law; he had hoped to practise at the bar, but a lifelong hearing impediment meant he had to settle for a job with the prominent solicitors Allen, Allen & Hemsley. As a member of parliament, he frequently had to plead with the speaker for absolute silence so he could hear the debates.

In his youth he was very much the young man about town, as well as the race track and the ballroom. The Sydney social whirl included a regular diet of conservative politics. But it was not until after the war, in which McMahon's hearing problems confined him to home duties, that he started to consider it as a career. Discharged with the rank of major, he returned to the university to study economics and public administration, joined the newly formed Liberal Party and gained preselection for the seat of Lowe, which he won in 1949.

Unlike his contemporary John Gorton, he was quick to gain favour, and entered the ministry in 1951 in the junior portfolios of Navy and Air. In 1954 he was promoted to Social Services and in 1956, unexpectedly, to Primary Industry. This appointment resulted from McEwen's old portfolio of Commerce and Agriculture being divided; McEwen kept Commerce, which became Trade, and

McMahon was given Agriculture, which became Primary Industry.

It was expected that the younger man would run his new department with the instruction and advice of the older, but the city slicker quickly showed his independence and competence and made the new portfolio his own, at times in open conflict with McEwen. A major row over the reconstruction of the dairy industry laid the foundations for a long and bitter feud between the two which came to a head when, after a long stint in Labour and National Service, McMahon took over the Treasury in 1966, becoming deputy leader of his party after the retirement of Menzies.

Treasury and Trade were now locked in an ongoing battle which revived the free trade versus protectionism split of pre-federation days. With the backing of Holt, McMahon won a series of major confrontations with McEwen, culminating in an acrimonious brawl over the devaluation of the currency. This intensified immediately before Holt's death and McEwen's refusal to serve in any government led by McMahon was the inevitable consequence.

With Gorton in charge, positions were reversed; the new Prime Minister rightly suspected that McMahon was white-anting him from the beginning, and turned to McEwen as insurance against the threat. After the 1969 election Gorton felt powerful enough to remove McMahon from his Treasury portfolio, leaving him to languish in External Affairs, which he finally freed of its colonial overtones by renaming it Foreign Affairs. But by now McEwen's veto had been removed, leaving McMahon free to campaign openly against Gorton.

He had also removed the last stumbling block to his being seen as an acceptable candidate for the top job. Since his youth he had been known as a confirmed bachelor, with all the innuendo that phrase entails; in parliament Gough Whitlam had even called him an old queen. But in 1965, at the age of fifty-seven, he married a much younger Sydney socialite named Sonia Hopkins. The rumours persisted, and as late as 1972 a Gay Liberation campaigner, David Widdup, stood for McMahon's seat of Lowe under the slogan: "Vote for the poofter who lives in the electorate." But in McMahon's Bellevue Hill mansion the marriage seemed a happy one and resulted in three children.

Sonia was to prove a considerable asset during McMahon's short regime. Not long after becoming leader, McMahon made a ceremonial visit to Washington. At the welcoming banquet hosted by President Nixon, Sonia descended the staircase in a canary yellow dress slit almost to the armpits; "Ravishing," gasped the president as McMahon described how he had wooed his bride by crooning to her the song "Fascination", which the band was coincidentally playing. Taking the speaker's stand, he threw away his prepared notes and declaimed: "I take as my text a few familiar words that there comes a time in the life of man in the flood of time that taken at the flood leads on to fortune." In the backroom where the media were watching the event on closed circuit, an Australian journalist groaned: "God, I wish I were Italian."

After that it was hard to take him seriously. Back in Australia McMahon sought to go back to the Menzies era; he mended fences with the state premiers and the public service, removed Gorton and his most vocal supporters from the ministry, and threw himself into a punishing working schedule to try to control an economy in which both inflation and unemployment were rising ominously. He received little credit for his efforts either from the public or from his increasingly disillusioned colleagues. Once, when he lamented to the party room, "I sometimes think I must be my own worst enemy," Jim Killen, ousted from the Navy portfolio, replied fiercely: "Not while I'm alive."

His last bulwark was removed when Sir Frank Packer sold his flagship *Daily Telegraph* to the then Whitlam backer Rupert Murdoch. Packer rang the Prime Minister to give him the bad news. McMahon's wail of despair was audible across the room. Packer then handed the phone to Murdoch, who gave the assurance: "I can promise, Prime Minister, that we will be as fair to you as you deserve." Packer interjected: "If you do that, you'll murder him." And McMahon's bald, pointy head and huge ears were a cartoonist's delight. Killen said he looked like a Volkswagen with both doors open. By the time he went to the polls at the end of 1972, McMahon had become a figure of fun: Labor supporters were handing out badges bearing the devastating message: "Stop laughing at Billy."

His stint as Prime Minister was not memorable for any important legislation or lasting achievements. But he left office with good grace. It had been a brief but cheerful interlude and if he had done nothing else, he had proved beyond doubt that after twenty-three years in power, the coalition had definitely run out of puff and it was at last time for a change.

EDWARD GOUGH WHITLAM

OF THE MANY compliments paid to Gough Whitlam, one of the best came from Neville Wran. The acerbic NSW Premier summed up his friend and colleague thus: "It was said of Caesar Augustus that he found a Rome of brick and left it of marble. It can be said of Gough Whitlam that he found Sydney, Melbourne and Brisbane unsewered and left them fully flushed."

It was a line that delighted Whitlam, whose epic visions of reform were always firmly grounded in improving the quality of life. He began with the outhouse and reached for the stars.

His vision was both his strength and his undoing; few if any have come to the office with a more ambitious program or left it in more dramatic circumstances. He was Prime Minister for less than three years – not even a full constitutional term. In that short tenure he became a legendary figure, a hero and martyr to his followers, and a wrecker of demonic proportions to his foes. But none can deny his stature as the dominant politician of his times.

Edward Gough Whitlam was born in Kew, Victoria, in 1916. His father, Fred, worked in the crown solicitor's office, and was transferred to Sydney when Gough was five and thence to Canberra. Gough was educated at Knox Grammar and at both public and private schools in the new national capital. He then took up residence at St Paul's College at Sydney University, where he studied the classics.

The family was serious about education; after dinner, Fred was known to issue volumes of the *Encyclopaedia Britannica* to his children and guests for a little light reading. Gough was a serious student but found time to gain a blue in rowing; he was later to say that the sport was an apt one for men in public life because you could face one way while going in the other.

He was also prominent in amateur theatrics and edited the literary magazine *Hermes*. And later, when he studied at the downtown law school, he revelled in what passed for café society; he was involved in a brief but torrid affair with the concert violinist Guila Bustabo but a year later met Margaret Dovey, whom he courted assiduously until they married in 1942.

In the meantime the war had put an end to his exuberant youth. Whitlam joined the Sydney University regiment in 1939 and after Pearl Harbor enlisted with the Royal Australian Air Force. He overcame chronic air-sickness to become a navigator and flew reconnaissance and bombing sorties out of Gove in northern Australia. In the process he was drawn into political activity; somewhat to the consternation of his superior officers he handed out pro-ALP material in the mess. Upon his discharge he joined the party.

His opponents later accused him of opportunism; they claimed he had only chosen Labor because it offered more chance of advancement than the Liberal Party. But there is plenty of evidence that he was by then firmly committed to the cause of social democracy and reform. While finishing his law degree he frequently lectured his fellow students on the need for constitutional change, a habit he never abandoned.

The Whitlams built a house in Cronulla, a southern suburb and a hotbed of left-wing radicalism. Within the local ALP the brash young lawyer was seen as a bit of a silvertail and a know-all; most of the members were more interested in revolution than the constitution. But they could not fault Whitlam's dedication and talent. He stood unsuccessfully for Sutherland Shire Council and for state parliament, and his efforts during those campaigns were rewarded with a narrow win in the preselection ballot for the safe seat of Werriwa in Sydney's west. When the sitting member Bert Lazzarini retired in 1952, Whitlam entered parliament in a by-election.

His course was set. But once again he found himself something of an outsider in Bert Evatt's diverse caucus. He avoided the bar and the billiard room and immersed himself in studying every aspect of policy; at a time when politics was a much more impromptu craft than it has become, Whitlam kept files on everything. Les Haylen christened him "the young brolga".

In the early days Whitlam was considered a bit of a lefty, largely because of his progressive approach to foreign affairs; but in campaign work he showed his pragmatism by concentrating on the relevant issues for individual seats. As a result he attracted support from many of his fellow backbenchers, especially the younger ones; the other serious leadership contenders – Arthur Calwell, Reg Pollard and Eddie Ward –

were already in their sixties and Whitlam represented the new generation.

However he remained loyal to Evatt and supported his leader through the split. He was elected to the caucus executive in 1958 and, when Evatt resigned in 1960, surprisingly beat Ward to become Calwell's deputy. The 1961 election almost saw Labor back in government, but Menzies regained the lost ground in 1963, partly through targeting the "thirty-six faceless men" of Labor's federal conference, who set the policy the parliamentarians were pledged to follow. Whitlam set out to rectify the problem by reforming the party structure, and as a result he spent the next eight years more or less constantly at war with the Labor machine.

The left had the numbers at both the conference and on the twelve-man executive which ran the party between conferences. Whitlam's campaign led to him being seen as a creature of the right, particularly when he took up the cause of state aid for private schools, one of the left's traditional bugbears. And of course he sought the support of the right, which controlled the NSW branch, to force the powerbrokers of the left to accept reform. But in policy terms he remained an internationalist free-thinker, a prototype progressive. In contrast Arthur Calwell, who sought refuge with the traditional left in his home state of Victoria, was a conservative Catholic advocate of White Australia. Such are the accidents of history.

With the aid of the party's new federal secretary, Cyril Wyndham, Whitlam gained some ground but progress was painfully slow, and in 1966 he decided on a direct assault in the manner which became his political trademark: crash through or crash. He launched a blistering attack on the party leadership and in particular those he called "the twelve witless men" of the federal executive. They immediately charged him with gross disloyalty and it appeared that the numbers were there to have him expelled, or at least suspended; but at the last minute he was saved by the delegates from Queensland, where he had recently led a successful campaign to win a by-election for Labor.

Yet he was still treated with suspicion, especially when he failed to give Calwell unequivocal backing for his promise to immediately withdraw all Australian troops from Vietnam; he regarded the policy as both impractical and unacceptable. The voters agreed; Labor was massively defeated at the 1966 election. Calwell, now a three-time loser, reluctantly resigned and Whitlam achieved what he had once vaingloriously described as his destiny: the leadership of the Labor Party.

He still had his enemies, particularly among the intransigent left-wing controllers of the Victorian branch. He accused them of constructing "a philosophy of failure which saw in defeat a form of justification and proof of the purity of our principles". And he added scornfully: "Certainly the impotent are pure."

Whitlam was eager for power, and once again resolved to crash through. When in 1968 the federal executive sought to reassert its authority, he resigned the party leadership, challenging the caucus either to sack him or back him. A challenge came from the charismatic left-winger Jim Cairns; the then advertising man Phillip Adams ran the anti-Whitlam campaign under the slogan "Whose party is it? His or ours?" Whitlam won the caucus vote, but it was a close thing: 38 to 32. The party was not yet entirely his.

But it swung behind him after the 1969 election. Running the campaign almost single-handed, Whitlam achieved a swing to Labor of almost 7 per cent, winning 17 seats in the process. Only in Victoria did the party not gain ground and in the following year the reform process finally reconstituted the state branch. In the period leading up to 1972 Whitlam seemed unstoppable. The climax was his visit to China, which fortuitously coincided with that of the US secretary of state Henry Kissinger, who was preparing the way for President Nixon. Whitlam represented the future; McMahon, leading the crumbling remnants of the Menzies era, was the past.

Whitlam and his followers could now start serious preparation for government, which meant "The Program". The aim of the program was to modernise the country, but it had the necessary corollary of modernising the Labor Party. For most of its life the party platform had been built around the pledge to nationalise the means of production, distribution and exchange. To the practical politicians this no longer meant wall-to-wall socialism; Chifley's experience with the banks had shown that was not only unsaleable but impractical. But the mantra of centralised public ownership still held sway. Whitlam was determined to adapt this concept to the circumstances of the day.

He liked to refer to the existing party platform as the Old Testament and to his program as the New Testament. Certainly it was a comprehensive list of objectives: huge changes to the health, education and welfare systems were at its heart along with consumer protection, equal pay, a family court and land rights for Aboriginal Australians, among many other social reforms. Unfortunately the more general question of economic management received rather less attention, so when the first unforeseen rise in international oil prices and the consequent leap in inflation struck, Whitlam and his inexperienced team were totally unprepared.

Labor had hit the ground running after an unexpectedly narrow victory in 1972. The hoopla surrounding the "It's Time" campaign and the demoralisation of the McMahon government (whose pathetic reply was "Not Yet") had prepared the faithful for a landslide but the majority was just 8 seats – comfortable, but hardly a resounding mandate for change.

Nonetheless the new government treated it as such. Whitlam and his deputy, Lance Barnard, were sworn into office holding all twenty-five portfolios between them and went to work; they did not even wait for a full ministry to be elected, let alone for parliament to convene. Such was the pace of change that the newspapers started running daily columns headed "What the government did yesterday"; they often ran to several hundred words. When the new ministers took office, they vied with each other to keep up with the leaders; the impression was of a government not only in a hurry, but one living on borrowed time.

And when the first crunch came, Whitlam made it clear that the Program was to take priority over prudent economic management. Some ministers urged caution. When Clyde Cameron tried to make sense of the altered circumstances, Whitlam swept him aside with the comment: "What would an ex-shearer know about the economy?" Cameron replied pointedly: "As much as an ex–classical Greek scholar," but the point was that neither of them knew much. To be fair, they were not alone; governments around the world were caught short by the oil-price shock.

It was clear by the start of 1974 that the government, while still well on top of its opponents, was becoming rattled. As usual, Whitlam took the bold course. Much of his legislation had been rejected or delayed by a hostile Senate. A half-Senate election was due; with a little manipulation, Labor might gain control. The manipulation involved removing the DLP leader, Vince Gair, by offering him the ambassadorship to Ireland; but the plan went horribly wrong and the opposition under Bill Snedden took the unprecedented step of blocking supply.

Whitlam called a double dissolution election, which Labor won, but still without control of the Senate. He did, however, get key legislation passed at a joint sitting of parliament. Medibank, the predecessor of Medicare, came into being as a lasting legacy. But the government was now starting to look vulnerable, with the economy clearly deteriorating. Whitlam wanted a big circuit-breaker: "Something like the Suez Canal," he mused to a dumbstruck cabinet.

And he nearly got it through the heady ambition of Rex Connor, his Minister for Minerals and Energy, who proposed building a gas and oil pipeline grid across the entire continent. The problem was affordability, so an inner circle of ministers hatched a plan to borrow $4 billion from the newly rich nations who formed the Organization of Petroleum Exporting Countries. If it had succeeded quickly, the move would have been accounted a triumph. As it was, it developed into an ongoing scandal, as sinister figures with white shoes and green sunglasses emerged from the shadows making improbable offers which were never fulfilled. In parliament the opposition, with the aid of leaks from the Treasury which had been horrified by the whole idea, had a picnic.

The government was unable, and in some cases unwilling, to extricate itself. Eventually Whitlam was forced to sack both Connor and the Treasurer, Jim Cairns – who was already embroiled in a damaging scandal involving his secretary, Junie Morosi – for having misled the parliament. He had previously forced the resignation of the speaker, Jim Cope, and the brilliant but accident-prone Attorney-General Lionel Murphy and Whitlam's longstanding deputy Lance Barnard had both left parliament to take up government appointments as a judge and ambassador respectively. Whitlam made a last-ditch effort to hold things together through an extensive cabinet reshuffle, and the new Treasurer, Bill Hayden, brought down a budget which finally recognised the economic realities, but it was too little and too late. The sacking of Connor gave the new opposition leader, Malcolm Fraser, the reprehensible circumstance he had been waiting for, and once again the opposition blocked supply.

This time Whitlam resolved to tough it out. He was convinced that the Governor-General he had personally appointed, Sir John Kerr, could be trusted to take his advice. And he was convinced that sooner or later some of the opposition senators would buckle rather than force an unprecedented economic and political crisis. After three weeks of a somewhat hysterical stand-off, it seemed he would be proved right; the budget was working, the government's standing was improving and by all accounts a handful of senators were wavering. And then, on 11 November 1975, Kerr changed the rules and sacked the government, installing Fraser as the unelected Prime Minister. Stunned, Whitlam went back to the Lodge and ate a large steak for lunch.

Meanwhile, unaware that they were now officially in opposition, the Labor senators voted to pass supply, and although the House of Representatives voted "no confidence" in Fraser, Kerr refused to receive the Speaker bearing this advice and prorogued parliament; this was the point at which he tore up the rule book altogether. It was a clear signal to the watching public that Whitlam must have done something terribly wrong, even if they couldn't say what it was; after all, his own Governor-General would not have sacked him if this were not the case.

There was talk of a national strike, but the fear was that if one took place, Kerr, as the titular commander-in-chief, would call out the armed forces; the risk of civil strife was too horrible to contemplate. Whitlam and Labor went, but not quietly. The campaign that followed was bitter and unremitting, but inevitably Fraser, with the vice-regal imprimatur, triumphed. Whitlam offered to resign the party leadership but was persuaded to stay on; after another crushing defeat in 1977 he handed over to Bill Hayden.

In retirement he maintained his rage against Kerr but was reconciled with Fraser, frequently appearing on the same platform as his old adversary in support of shared ideals such as press diversity and republicanism. After Labor regained office in 1983, Bob Hawke appointed him Australia's ambassador to UNESCO, a post ironically occupied briefly by Kerr shortly after the dismissal. As always, Whitlam filled the sinecure with diligence and enthusiasm. And of course he remained active in the cause of constitutional reform.

The achievements of his short-lived government were enormous; many of them are now taken for granted as part of the social framework, but in their day they were considered radical, even revolutionary. Medicare remains the most obvious, but equal pay for women, consumer protection laws, no-fault divorce, Aboriginal land rights, free university education, legislation to protect the environment and national heritage, acceptance of international laws and treaties, and many lesser innovations were all genuine breakthroughs. But the most notable thing about them is that they were brought about within the parliamentary system as part of a well-thought-out program. Always the rational optimist, Whitlam believed that democracy could be trusted – that in the end decency and good sense would prevail. He embraced political power not as an end in itself, but for what it could accomplish for the betterment of society; he governed with relish and he governed with style. Whatever the faults of his administration, it was never boring.

And the same could be said of his retirement. He particularly enjoyed his time as chairman of the National Gallery. On one occasion the director, Betty Churcher, informed him of a plan – fortunately aborted – that would have made him appear to walk across water to the opening of a special exhibition. "Comrade," said Whitlam, "that would not have been possible. The stigmata have not yet healed." Self-mockery, undoubtedly; but to those who experienced the exhilarating roller-coaster ride of his time as Prime Minister after twenty-three stultifying years in opposition, he had indeed appeared a political Messiah.

JOHN MALCOLM FRASER

FOR OLDER AUSTRALIANS there are two Malcolm Frasers.

The first: the remote and remorseless squire of Nareen, the capital-L Liberal ruthless right-winger with the face of an Easter Island statue and the fist of iron to smash the unions, the ruthless destroyer of parliamentary convention and anything and anyone that stood in the way of his lust for power. And then the second: the small-l liberal caring humanitarian, friend of indigenous Australians, oppressed Asian refugees and black Africans, the multicultural republican conservationist who all too humanly lost his trousers in a Memphis hotel.

Surely they can't both be right; but according to the man himself, they are. It was not John Malcolm Fraser who changed; it was the world, and particularly the Australian political scene, which changed around him.

He was born in Toorak in 1930. The Frasers were well known in Victoria; Malcolm Fraser's grandfather, an immigrant from Nova Scotia, had been a senator in the first Commonwealth parliament and as a speculator and later an extensive landowner had made the family wealthy. Nonetheless Malcolm's childhood, on one of the family properties near Deniliquin in the Riverina, was a harsh and lonely one. Recalling it later he said the most frightening experience of his life was when his father pretended to abandon him on an island amid rising flood waters, and the funniest when his father tipped his mother off the back of a sulky into a mud puddle.

He spent his first ten years doing menial farm labour, although he was sent to school at Glamorgan, which later became part of Geelong Grammar. In 1943 the family bought Nareen, a prestigious property in the western districts of Victoria, and Fraser was sent to Melbourne Grammar as a boarder. He is remembered as a shy child, and a not particularly diligent scholar. Nonetheless his father persuaded the authorities at his alma mater, Magdalen College at Oxford, to accept him, where he completed a course in modern greats.

Once again, he left no lasting impression; one of his tutors described him as "a colonial drongo". But he did develop an interest in politics, centred on a distrust of socialism as a means of delivering genuine progress. He later described his position at this time as "idealistic conservatism".

Back in Australia, the choice had to be made between a career on the farm or one in politics. Unsurprisingly Fraser decided politics was more exciting and joined the Liberal Party. He stood for the federal seat of Wannon in 1954 and lost, but won it comfortably in the following year. At the age of twenty-five, he was by far the youngest member of the

Commonwealth parliament. Perhaps for that reason he had to wait a long time for promotion and when it came under Harold Holt, it was only to the junior Army Ministry – admittedly a sensitive post at the time of conscription for Vietnam.

Worried that he was being left behind his generational rivals from Victoria – Don Chipp, Billy Snedden and Peter Howson, and even newcomers like Phillip Lynch and Andrew Peacock – he started cultivating his own clique around the Senate leader, John Gorton. Fraser was a leading figure in the group that was preparing Gorton for a challenge to Holt before the latter's death and ran his campaign for the leadership after it. Gorton rewarded him with his own former portfolio of Education and Science, in which Fraser greatly increased funding for both tertiary education and private secondary schools. After the 1969 election Gorton moved him to Defence, giving him the position of seniority and influence he had coveted.

Throughout his career Fraser thrived on crisis, and when one was not occurring naturally, he set out to create it. In 1970, when rioting erupted in Papua New Guinea, he clashed with colleagues over whether to call out the Pacific Islands Regiment to restore order. And then in 1971 he provoked a showdown over civil aid in Vietnam with the new Army Minister, Andrew Peacock. Gorton backed Peacock, and after a campaign fought largely through selective press briefings, Fraser turned on his patron and resigned, accusing Gorton of gross disloyalty. The resulting turmoil led to Gorton's own resignation, the first of Fraser's three decisive coups.

After a cooling-off period on the backbench, he was forced to make do with his old portfolio of Education and

Science, Defence having been appropriated by Gorton. He held it until the change of government in 1972. In opposition Billy Snedden, sensing a potential threat, attempted to sideline Fraser by making him spokesman for Primary Industry; Fraser responded by making it clear to all and sundry that he was the party's natural leader, the only figure in opposition who could take Prime Minister Gough Whitlam head on. Within the party room he was widely disliked and distrusted, but the coalition was desperate to regain government, so they reluctantly fell in behind him. In 1975 Snedden, assailed by Whitlam from the front and Fraser from the rear, eventually succumbed to Fraser's second coup.

By then the Labor government was clearly beyond recovery; all Fraser had to do was wait for power to fall into his lap at the next election. But he was too impatient for that; once more he provoked a crisis by blocking the government's supply through a Senate majority conferred following a breach of convention by the Queensland Premier, Joh Bjelke-Petersen. In the frantic days which followed, Fraser alone stayed calm; he was convinced, either through prescience or foreknowledge, that the Governor-General, Sir John Kerr, would sack Whitlam and his government; and so it proved. Fraser won a record majority at the subsequent election. His third coup had been the most spectacularly successful of all.

But the conservative counter-revolution his followers expected failed to eventuate. Although the Liberals had a majority in their own right and control of the Senate, Fraser decided to abandon the habit of a lifetime and take the route of cautious conservatism. His closeness to the Country Party strongmen Doug Anthony, Ian Sinclair and Peter Nixon meant that he eschewed the economic rationalism urged on him by some Liberals and by the Treasury; as a farmer himself, he was an instinctive protectionist. And although he moved to rein in some of the Whitlam government's spending spree, the cuts were nowhere near as ruthless as his supporters had expected; some, like the sale of the government-owned merry-go-round in Canberra's civic centre, were simply petty.

Even after he was returned in 1977 with another thumping majority he temporised; his only really tough policies involved a series of confrontations with the trade unions, which had little lasting effect, and an unsuccessful attempt to force Australia's sporting bodies to boycott the Moscow Olympic Games. Most importantly the economy, whose critical state had been the ostensible reason for his third and final coup, stubbornly failed to respond to the remedy offered by Treasury, which was to let unemployment rise as a means of reducing inflation. Instead, stagflation – low growth and continuing high inflation – set in. And the government's responses were erratic, even desperate. Fraser introduced tax indexation, then rescinded it; he gave tax cuts, but grabbed them back. By the 1980 election the government was teetering and only a last-minute scare about capital gains tax saved it after an effective campaign by the new Labor leader Bill Hayden.

Moreover, 1980 saw the election to parliament of the immensely popular Bob Hawke, who made no secret of his own ambition for Hayden's, and thence Fraser's, job. By the end of 1982 inflation and unemployment were both rising again and Hawke was poised for a coup of his own. Fraser was ready to call an early election to pre-empt him, but his always suspect health intervened. By the time he got round to visiting the Governor-General in February next year, Hawke had beaten him by a matter of hours. The election which followed was no contest. Fraser's normally stony face crumbled into tears as he acknowledged the massive defeat.

To his followers on the right of politics his had been wasted years; the opportunity to push through uncompromising free-market reforms had been lost. Fraser, as his favourite author, the American ideologue Ayn Rand, once said of him disparagingly, had not been selfish enough. Yet seen from a different perspective, the record was a truly impressive one. Fraser had vastly increased the immigration program, including in it some 56,000 Vietnamese refugees, of whom 2000 were boat people. He had introduced a system of family allowances and Freedom of Information legislation. He had implemented Whitlam's bill for Northern Territory Aboriginal land rights, saved Fraser Island from sand-mining and ended whaling in Australia. In foreign affairs he had led the international campaign against the racist regimes in South Africa and Rhodesia (Zimbabwe). And perhaps most significantly, he had set up the SBS multicultural broadcasting network and founded the Institute of Multicultural Affairs. He was later to claim the encouragement and recognition of a genuinely multicultural Australia as his finest achievement.

It was a record of which any leftist Prime Minister might be proud, but Malcolm Fraser? Yes, Malcolm Fraser, who in retirement founded the Australian branch of Care International and later became the organisation's president; Malcolm Fraser, whom Bob Hawke appointed to the Eminent Persons Group to help manage transition in South Africa, and backed for the post of Commonwealth Secretary-General; Malcolm

Fraser, who appeared on numerous platforms with his old adversary Gough Whitlam in support of such causes as media diversity and republicanism; Malcolm Fraser, who became increasingly critical of his party over such issues as the conduct of the Iraq war, the imprisonment in Guantanamo Bay of Australians David Hicks and Mamdouh Habib and, above all, the government's treatment of asylum seekers. His wife Tamie openly referred to John Howard as "that ghastly little racist".

The estrangement became complete when Tony Abbott took the party leadership in 2009. Fraser, who had been awarded life membership in 1976, formally resigned, saying that it was no longer a Liberal Party; it had become a Conservative Party and he could no longer relate to it. One Liberal frontbencher said he had become a "frothing-at-the-mouth leftie". And his appearance in 1986 in the foyer of a somewhat sleazy Memphis hotel in search of his trousers had certainly stripped away much of his former gravitas.

Fraser is famous for uttering the mantra of metaphysical pessimism, "Life wasn't meant to be easy"; in later years he justified it by pointing out that the full quotation, from George Bernard Shaw's play *Back to Methuselah*, reads: "Life is not meant to be easy, my child; but take courage: it can be delightful." However, when previously confronted by a reporter seeking an explanation, he had replied simply: "Well, it wasn't, was it?" Certainly his early years had persuaded him of the truth of the dictum, and it could be said that in the course of his career he gave a lot of other people a pretty hard time too.

But it was a career of some achievement. Asked in 2003 how he thought history would remember him, he drew himself up to his full height and replied with a touch of his old arrogance: "Well, a great deal better than the Liberal Party does." Nearly a decade later, there was little doubt of that.

ROBERT JAMES LEE HAWKE

LIKE MOST POLITICIANS, Bob Hawke craved power; but more than that, he demanded affection.

Not for him the dictum of the emperor Tiberius, "Let them hate me as long as they fear me"; his entire career was based on his camaraderie with the electorate. Indeed, he more than once described his time as Prime Minister as "my love affair with the Australian public".

But just because he was a lover, it did not mean that he could not also be a fighter when the occasion demanded. Many an opponent, and not a few of his colleagues, discovered that he could be a dangerous man to cross. He seldom had to prove his toughness; first and foremost Hawke was the great persuader, having developed a talent for conciliation and mediation during his trade union days. And as a result, sheer persistence enabled him to drag his party away from some of its most sacred traditions and to lead one of the most radical reform governments since federation. Seldom has popularity been exploited to better effect.

Robert James Lee Hawke first announced that he was destined to be Prime Minister at the age of fifteen, but others had recognised the inevitability well before that. His father, Clem, was a Congregationalist minister in Bordertown in South Australia, and when his wife Ellie was pregnant in 1929, he noted that the family Bible fell open at Isaiah 9:6: "For unto us a child is born, a son is given; and the government shall be upon his shoulder." In addition Clem's brother Bert, who became Premier of Western Australia, was a close friend of John Curtin's, who was to become Bob Hawke's idol and role model. His path could hardly have been clearer.

The family moved to Perth and Hawke attended the prestigious Perth Modern School and then the University of Western Australia; he is remembered as a likeable and competent student but not a great scholar. Nonetheless he applied for and gained a Rhodes scholarship to Oxford, where he promptly distinguished himself by drinking a yard of beer in eleven seconds. He also completed a thesis on Australia's wage-fixing system, an unlikely subject for Oxford, but one that was to prove an excellent career move.

On his return to Australia in 1956 he married Hazel Masterson and accepted another scholarship, this time to do a PhD in arbitration law at the Australian National University in Canberra. He thrived in the political ambience of the national capital and soon became the student representative on the University Council. And he came to the notice of the Australian Council of Trade Unions (ACTU) president Albert Monk, who recruited him as a research officer. Hawke abandoned his studies and the family moved to Melbourne.

The blokey culture of the union movement centred around the John Curtin Hotel, where Hawke became something of a fixture. But he also carved out a reputation as a highly successful advocate before the Conciliation and Arbitration Commission, starting with a bravura appearance at the 1959 basic wage case. He joined the ALP and in 1963 ran for the federal seat of Corio without success; his real power base was in the industrial movement. He knew the law better than most of the judges and could argue with economists on their own ground. And he was a pre-eminent man of the people, one with whom the workers could identify – a keen punter and a highly competitive sportsman, on and off the field.

By 1969 he had become something of a national celebrity, and when Monk retired as ACTU president, Hawke, who had never held an elected office, stood against the long-serving secretary Harold Souter for the job. With the help of the left vote he scored a narrow victory and proceeded to expand and modernise the organisation, affiliating many previously hostile white-collar associations and even encouraging the arch-enemy, big business, to form partnerships with the unions. He was not by nature a militant; he always preferred negotiated settlements to strike action. Some traditional unionists saw this as timidity, but since Hawke consistently delivered improvements in wages and conditions, they had little support for their complaints. Politically he moved well to the right, becoming an uncritical supporter of both the United States and Israel. His previous allies on the left of the party found his alliance with two countries of whom they had always been suspicious both naïve and unacceptable.

But the more general worry within the ALP about Hawke concerned his drinking and womanising, both of which were of Olympic standard. His successful television appearances made him immensely popular with the general public, but the political professionals saw him as something of a loose cannon. However, by 1972 he was regarded as a Prime Minister in waiting and a possible rival to the ascendant Gough Whitlam. He certainly saw himself in that light. There was a celebrated occasion when, after a heavy drinking session, he presented himself with an overnight bag at the door of a woman known to be sympathetic to Labor politicians. The ACTU leader had a proposal he thought would be irresistible: "How would you like to be the mistress of the next Prime Minister of Australia?" To her credit, the woman did not miss a beat. "Oh, I don't think Margaret Whitlam would like that," she replied and firmly closed the door.

But the knockbacks, like the setbacks, were rare. In 1973 Hawke was elected president of the ALP and in the aftermath of the dismissal of 1975, when Hawke had resisted demands to call a national strike, Whitlam offered to stand down as leader if Hawke would take over. Hawke, to his later regret, temporised, and Whitlam withdrew an offer which in any case he had no power to make. When Whitlam resigned in 1977, Bill Hayden had established himself as the natural successor, but Hawke's ambition was by then revived. He consistently sought to dominate Hayden at party forums and their rivalry came to a head at the 1979 National Conference in Adelaide, where an argument between the two on industrial policy was resolved in Hayden's favour. Hawke saw it as a betrayal, and after many hours of heavy drinking declared to a group of journalists: "As far as Bill Hayden and I are concerned, Hayden is dead. As far as Bill Hayden and I are concerned, it's finished – he's a lying cunt with a limited future." Shortly afterwards his health gave way and he decided to lay off the grog.

There was an uneasy reconciliation between the two before the 1980 election, at which Hawke finally entered parliament, having publicly promised not to drink for as long as he was a member, a promise which was greeted with great scepticism by his colleagues, but which he kept. Labor very nearly won the poll and Hayden was back on top; Hawke had to bide his time. He inevitably became Labor's spokesman on Industrial Relations, but was a curiously restrained performer in the chamber; his only memorable performance was calling Prime Minister Malcolm Fraser a liar, and being allowed to get away with it by the Speaker, Bill Snedden.

With the help of his friends in the ACTU he was able to erode Hayden's support, and in 1982 made his first challenge. He lost, but ran it close, and with another election looming and the opinion polls showing him to be far more popular than either Fraser or Hayden, the party, desperate to regain office, eventually swung behind him. Hayden's close friend and supporter John Button persuaded the leader to stand aside and Hawke took the leadership hours before Fraser, in a last-ditch attempt to forestall him, called the election. The result was never in doubt; Fraser campaigned like a loser and Hawke treated the election as a victory parade. Hayden famously said that a drover's dog could have won it, and if he had remained as leader he would almost certainly have done so; but it is highly unlikely that he would have won three more. For Hawke, it all fell into place.

Part of his success was sheer luck. For much of his term in office the rivalry between Andrew Peacock and John Howard for the leadership of the Liberal Party meant that he seldom had to face a united opposition. And as a bonus, 1987 brought the preposterous "Joh for PM" campaign in which the eccentric Queensland Premier Bjelke-Petersen totally destroyed whatever chance John Howard, then in the chair, might have had.

Yet to an extent Hawke made his own luck. Having been elected on the slogan of recovery, reconciliation and reconstruction, his first move was to call a summit meeting of business and union leaders, together with other stakeholders in the economy, to try and achieve some form of national consensus. The summit was greeted with some cynicism by hardened professionals; the NSW Premier Neville Wran had advised a pre-election meeting of his colleagues, "Delegates, it's all very well to go on with all this spiritual stuff, but if the greedy bastards out there wanted spiritualism they'd join the fucking Hare Krishna." So the meeting threw in the promise of tax cuts.

But in fact the summit was successful, fixing in place the Prices and Incomes Accord that was to be the centrepiece of a stable and predictable economy. As well as maintaining his important union contacts, Hawke opened up unprecedented lines of communication with business; extraordinarily, key figures such as Kerry Packer actually endorsed a Labor government. And Hawke had the benefit of a ministry which, in his first term at least, was the most talented in living memory.

All these factors gave him and his Treasurer, the energetic Paul Keating, the firm base from which to implement a program of economic reform that a less secure government would never have dared contemplate. The key reforms were the floating of the Australian dollar and the deregulation of financial markets, including the admission of foreign banks.

From these flowed the unwinding of tariff protection and subsidies and the privatisation of key institutions, including Qantas Airways and even the Commonwealth Bank. For any government these changes would have been revolutionary; coming from the ALP they were almost unimaginable, smashing as they did icons that the party had held sacred since its creation almost a century earlier. So dominant were Hawke and Keating that the unions were even persuaded to accept a form of enterprise bargaining, dropping the collective approach which had been their very reason for being.

More generally there were far-reaching changes to the tax system, including the introduction of a fringe benefit tax and a capital gains tax, the latter partly offset by dividend imputation. These reforms stopped at the final hurdle; Keating had favoured a consumption tax, but Hawke, pressed by the unions, vetoed it. There was some opposition from within the party, but not enough to slow the momentum. The reforms of the Hawke–Keating years are now held up by both sides of politics to have been both ground-breaking and necessary, laying the foundations for Australia's role in the emerging global economy.

They also became the basis for an ongoing rivalry between the protagonists. What had been a balanced and fruitful partnership became a confrontation between the old bull and the young bull. Keating had always assumed that Hawke would step aside at some point to give him his own turn in the Lodge. As time went by, Hawke became increasingly reluctant to set a timetable. Eventually Keating insisted on a written agreement, in front of witnesses, that Hawke would step aside after the 1990 election; but when the time came, Hawke reneged, claiming that Keating had been disloyal by comparing himself to the great Placido Domingo in a speech to the Press Gallery at their annual dinner.

Keating mounted a challenge which Hawke easily saw off, and Keating retired to the backbench; but his very presence was a baleful influence. Beset by personal problems (Hawke's daughter Roslyn had become a heroin addict, as he tearfully admitted on television, and his marriage was under considerable stress) his previously impervious political grip began to fail. With the country dipping into recession the new opposition leader, John Hewson, announced a detailed economic policy called "Fightback!" which the government had trouble countering. And Keating made it clear that he intended to persevere with his destabilising campaign unless and until the party made him leader. At the end of 1991 they succumbed and Labor dumped its longest-serving and most successful Prime Minister.

Bob Hawke had surpassed all expectations. The hard-drinking larrikin who many had thought too shallow and too self-centred to lead his factionalised party had ensured his place in Labor's pantheon. The economic reforms remain his crowning achievement, but his government was also active in more traditional Labor areas. Medibank, allowed to languish under Fraser, was triumphantly reborn as Medicare. Social welfare was improved and communications policy brought up to date. And in later years Hawke turned his attention back to Aboriginal Affairs.

He had kept his promise to give up drinking, but had maintained his interest in women, and in particular in his biographer Blanche d'Alpuget, with whom he conducted a lengthy, if discreet, affair; shortly after he retired from parliament, following his defeat by Keating, he and Hazel divorced and he married Blanche. He also embarked on a successful business career. The Hawkes, now disrespectfully rechristened B1 and B2, became a fixture on Sydney's A-list. He was already estranged from his children; he had split with his son Stephen over the issue of uranium mining, he had never been close to Susan, and Roslyn had taken up drugs. And his endless squabble with Keating over who was entitled to the major credit for his government's reforms continued to fester.

He was no longer the popular idol he had once been. But the Silver Bodgie, as he was more or less affectionately known, no longer needed public adulation. He could honestly say that, like his hero John Curtin, he had surmounted his personal flaws to become one of his country's great political achievers, a leader with an honoured place in his party's history. Even for an ego like Bob Hawke's, that was enough.

PAUL JOHN **KEATING**

IF AUSTRALIAN POLITICS operated a star system, Paul Keating would be top of the bill.

We have had many notable thespians among our leaders – Billy Hughes and Gough Whitlam, with their utterly contrasting styles, come immediately to mind. But no Prime Minister since federation has had the electrifying performance skills of the boy from Bankstown. In one of his many bids for the job he promised to add "a touch of excitement", and that was one promise he delivered in spades.

Even in retirement, his occasional television appearances kept viewers on the edge of their seats: what devastating put-down could they expect this evening? But it is frequently forgotten that behind the great entertainer there dwelt a serious and driven politician, indeed something of a visionary. His time as Treasurer and then, briefly, as Prime Minister was one of very substantial achievement.

Paul John Keating was born in the Sydney suburb of Bankstown in 1944. His family could be described as tribal

Irish Catholic; father Matt, a boilermaker, had risen from being a trade union delegate to running his own business and employing some 200 workers, but he remained welded to the Labor Party. Paul Keating was handing out leaflets and doing other election work while still at school at De La Salle College, and when he left after gaining his intermediate certificate his father inducted him into the party as soon as he turned fifteen, the minimum age allowed.

This was the time of the split, and Labor politics, especially for Catholics, was a turbulent and divisive business. Keating learned the toughness needed to survive at an early age. In the next few years he held a variety of jobs: he briefly attended night school to study electrical engineering, was a clerk with the Sydney County Council and joined some mates as a share farmer. He also managed a rock group called the Ramrods, whom, he later boasted, he took from nowhere to total obscurity.

But his eyes were firmly fixed on politics: he spent many hours sitting at the feet of the great Labor renegade Jack Lang, who taught him both ideology and tactics. By the age of eighteen he was chairman of the ALP State Youth Council, with the network of supporters he needed to gain preselection for the seat of Banks. He thought he had that sewn up, but a redistribution switched his home to neighbouring Blaxland, firmly in the grasp of an established local member. Nonetheless, Keating won the preselection. A subsequent ALP inquiry uncovered serious irregularities in the voting, but by then it was too late: Keating had entered parliament with a 7 per cent swing at the 1969 election and was firmly ensconced as the youngest member of the House of Representatives.

He used the Whitlam years to establish himself as an up-and-comer; commentators noted his carefully groomed Italianate appearance (from the start he was a snappy dresser) and inferred that behind it lay a Machiavelli lusting for power. Whitlam singled him out for praise and suggested that he should go back to school and do a university degree, but the brash young newcomer was not interested. "What for? Then I'd be like you," he retorted to his startled leader. On another occasion he told Whitlam impertinently: "You need me more than I'll ever need you." He was determined to be his own man.

He was eventually given the junior portfolio of Northern Australia in 1975, only to be told by Whitlam three weeks later that he was sacked. "What for?" asked the bewildered Minister and was coldly informed: "We've all been sacked."

Keating used the opposition years wisely. He asked for and was given the shadow portfolio of Minerals and Energy, previously held by the legendary Rex "The Strangler" Connor, who had replaced Jack Lang as Keating's political mentor during his time in parliament. He quickly built it into a formidable power base and became one of the leaders of the right-wing faction. In 1979 he became president of the NSW branch of the ALP. However, he supported his leader, the leftish Bill Hayden, against the insurgent Bob Hawke until almost the last gasp. Desperate to retain his backing Hayden appointed him shadow Treasurer, and in the interests of stability Hawke let him keep the job in spite of the more obvious and long-standing claims of Hawke's own protégé Ralph Willis. Such are the accidents that make history.

Keating had no economic background, but was a quick and willing learner at the hands of Treasury officials. By the middle of 1983 he was ready to defy the department's formidable secretary, John Stone, and float the Australian dollar. This was the first of a wave of economic reforms which overthrew Labor tradition. During this period Keating became close to the astute and influential ACTU secretary Bill Kelty, without whose support the government would have faced an open revolt from the unions. As it was, the changes went through surprisingly smoothly, so much so that an international right-wing money magazine anointed Keating "Finance Minister of the Year". He later claimed that he had a natural talent for economics, that he could play the economy like a violin. His colleagues put this down to typical Keating bravado, but once he felt he had mastered the brief he was both innovative and daring in his management of it. For better or worse he was seen as the driving force behind the changes. In time this was to have its downside; after he had christened the downturn of the '90s "the recession we had to have" he, rather than Hawke, was to cop the blame for it. But in the early years it was all positive; Keating embraced the role with a gusto that infected the public. For the moment at least they were enjoying the ride.

By now Keating had moved his family to Canberra; in 1975 he had married his wife, Annita, a Dutch air hostess he had met on an overseas trip. With their three young children they rented a pleasant house in a garden suburb where Keating garaged his Mercedes Benz coupé. He had well and truly left behind his working-class roots and was developing a taste for the finer things in life, including Italian tailoring, French first-empire antiques and the music of Gustav Mahler. But there was still more than a hint of the Bankstown boy. The then Arts Minister Barry Cohen recalled the time when the two were sharing a rug in the VIP section of the Sydney Opera Company's Opera in the Park concert. Munching sesame-seed chicken and sipping Bollinger, the Treasurer confided to his companion: "Hey Bazza, this beats being in opposition, eh? If we were, we'd be up the back chewing on a Mars Bar."

Labor won the 1984 election and the economic reforms continued; Keating claimed to be the mover and shaker behind them and now saw himself not just as Hawke's inevitable successor but as an equal, even the true leader. He regarded the Prime Minister's refusal to back his plans for a consumption tax as an act of cowardice and betrayal, and started mustering support. However, his impatience was seen as arrogance and his lifestyle told against him. He was now making extensive investments in business and property; his partnership in a piggery was considered particularly inappropriate, as was his friendship with the colourful property developer Warren Anderson. Hawke advised him to spend more time with ordinary Australians. Keating replied contemptuously that leadership was about more than tripping over television cables at shopping centres and that when the time came he could "throw the switch to vaudeville".

He was still well short of the numbers to challenge Hawke in the party room. Labor won the 1987 election, and Keating exacted a promise, made in front of witnesses, that Hawke would step down after the 1990 election. He then promised publicly not to challenge. But the good times were coming to an end; the country was drifting into recession and the government's hold on office was precarious. Labor survived in 1990 with the help of Green preferences, but Hawke refused to go, giving as his reason a speech Keating had made to the Press Gallery's annual dinner in which he said that Australia had never produced a great leader; Hawke took it personally. Keating challenged unsuccessfully in April 1991 and retired to the backbench, a divisive and destabilising presence which clearly rattled Hawke. In December he challenged again and the caucus reluctantly decided there was no alternative.

Paul Keating became Prime Minister with a public approval rating of just 17 per cent. The lack of public popularity did nothing to dampen his enthusiasm for the job. He immediately set about implementing what he called the big picture: this included making Australia a republic, reconciliation between indigenous and non-indigenous Australians, and developing the Asia Pacific Economic Co-operation forum started by Hawke to integrate Australia more firmly into its region.

He made a solid start to each of these aims, but was unable to follow through. The republic push faltered when Keating presumed to touch the Queen during a royal visit, an incident for which the English tabloids dubbed him "The Lizard of Oz". A moving speech in which he accepted blame for the wrongs done to Aboriginals failed to resonate with most white Australians, who resented the implication that they were personally guilty of the crimes of the past. And his conversion to Asia was confusing to those who recalled that a few years before he had dismissed it as "the place you fly over on your way to Europe".

But if the public did not warm to him, he was able to dominate the parliament in a way that Hawke never had. Keating had scorned Andrew Peacock's previous attempt at a comeback with the line "A soufflé doesn't rise twice." Now he called Peacock's successor, John Hewson, a "feral abacus" and launched a savage attack on the centrepiece of his Fightback! program, the GST – quite a feat of chutzpah considering the fact that he had been a passionate advocate of just such a tax seven years previously. But it worked; against all expectations Keating won the 1993 election, declaring it "one for the true believers ... the sweetest victory of all".

And for most of 1994 it seemed that he really had cemented his position. The Liberals replaced Hewson with Alexander Downer, whom even most of his colleagues considered a joke. Keating, in contrast, looked almost statesmanlike, especially when he successfully concluded a mammoth negotiation to produce a satisfactory outcome to the High Court's Mabo ruling, which had found Aboriginal Australians retained certain forms of land title. He also implemented a large job-creation and retraining program and laid the basis for universal superannuation as a partial solution to the problem of an ageing population. There was a feeling that he might, in spite of everything, break through.

All that changed at the start of 1995, when John Howard, the last man standing, regained the Liberal leadership. Keating's loathing of Howard included and transcended the man's policy, politics and personality; it was not rational but visceral. An example came with the assassination of Israeli Prime Minister Yitzhak Rabin; Keating refused to allow Howard to share his VIP flight to the funeral. On his return he spoke movingly of his time in Jerusalem: "You can see where Christ walked on his way to the crucifixion." Then someone mentioned Howard. "I think that little bastard's done us some damage," Keating said. An adviser suggested ignoring him. "I'm not going to ignore him, I'm going to drive an axe into his chest and lever his ribs apart," snarled the Prime Minister.

His language, especially in parliament, was becoming more extreme; in 1995 the opposition prepared a list of some of the names the Prime Minister had called them. It included: harlots, sleazebags, frauds, immoral cheats, blackguards, pigs, mugs, clowns, boxheads, criminal intellects, corporate crooks, brain-damaged loopy crims, stupid foulmouthed grub, piece of criminal garbage, stupid mindless dullards, alley cats, clot, fop, perfumed gigolos, harebrained, hillbilly, ninny, rustbucket, scum, scumbag, suckers, thugs, dimwits, dummies, swill, a pigsty, muck, rip-off merchants, gutless spivs, glib rubbish, tripe, drivel, vandals, stunned mullets and barnyard bullies, among many others. The public was amused but not edified.

Much was also made of Keating's allegedly opulent lifestyle: he purchased a new dining-room table for the Lodge and a set of Gould prints for the cabinet room. Such trivia would normally have gone unnoticed, but as always with Keating the incongruity of his contrasting styles made them news. And the economy still had not shaken itself out of "the recession we had to have"; interest rates had been too high for too long. As the 1996 election loomed, it was obvious that Labor was finally finished; 1993 had been not a rebirth but a reprieve. One Labor stalwart, Wayne Goss, remarked that ever since then the voters had been sitting on their verandahs, baseball bats in hand, waiting for Keating to come past.

And so it proved. He left office as he had gained it, unrepentant. "Thanks for the ride," he said as he farewelled his caucus colleagues. "The pleasure, the excitement, the thrills and spills – I wouldn't have missed it for quids." In retirement he built a successful career in business and, surprisingly, academia, becoming a Visiting Professor of Public Policy at the University of New South Wales. He separated from his wife in 1998, but remained close to his children, who all went on to successful careers.

In later years he became more retiring, concentrating his public life around art and architecture, but his occasional forays into politics were eagerly anticipated. And he had not lost his touch; he referred to Howard as "a desiccated coconut and pre-Copernican obscurantist", and to the Treasurer, Peter Costello, as "all tip and no iceberg". In 1997 he became the only former Prime Minister to decline the offer of an AC, the highest rank of the Order of Australia. And he holds another memorable first: what other Prime Minister has had a hit musical written about him?

JOHN WINSTON **HOWARD**

IF PAUL KEATING promised a touch of excitement, John Howard personified ordinariness. Indeed, his party's federal director, Lynton Crosby, once described him as "boring as batshit". His nicknames tell the story: "Honest John" was bestowed in irony after his period as Treasurer, and "Little Johnny" related not to his height but to his political vision.

But what he lacked in charisma he made up for in persistence. He was twenty-two years in parliament before he reached the top, but having become Prime Minister he clung to the job with a tenacity which has seldom been rivalled. In the end it cost his party government and him his own seat, but he remained unmoved. Having fought for so long he was not about to surrender the prize to those who lacked the courage to take him on.

John Winston Howard's inheritance was a conservative one and he never wavered from it. His father, Lyall, who owned a suburban service station in Sydney, had been a supporter of the quasi-Fascist New Guard, and when John was born in 1939 he gave his son the middle name of a Tory hero, although Churchill's time as great war leader was yet to come.

As a teenager Howard joined the Young Liberals and found an Australian idol in Robert Menzies; he would later look back on the Menzies years as a golden era in which people knew their place and did not challenge traditional values. When he became Prime Minister, one of his first acts was to get rid of the modern furniture in his Parliament House office and replace it with old-fashioned leather armchairs and the very desk at which Menzies had worked. In taste, as in policy, he was more of a reactionary than a genuine conservative.

Howard was educated at Canterbury Boys' High and worshipped at the local Methodist church, although he later moved to the more mainstream Anglican. His father died when he was sixteen, and he lived at home to look after his mother until 1971, when he married Janette Parker, another ambitious Young Liberal. He attended the off-campus Sydney University Law School, but only as a prelude to politics; he saw his upward path as being through the Liberal organisation, and by 1962 had achieved the presidency of the Young Liberals and was a member of the party's state executive, where he made some very useful contacts.

In 1963 he worked on a by-election campaign for Tom Hughes in Parkes against the senior Labor member Les Haylen. Howard produced pamphlets describing Haylen as "the Minister for Peking", and Hughes won the seat. In 1967 Howard won preselection for the state seat of Drummoyne but was defeated by the Labor incumbent; in 1972 he worked for Billy McMahon on his doomed campaign, but gained sufficient kudos to be preselected for the vacant federal seat of Bennelong, which he won in 1974.

He supported Malcolm Fraser against the then leader Bill Snedden, and after Fraser's coup in 1975 was rewarded with a place on the frontbench, becoming Minister for Business and Consumer Affairs in the new government. He used the portfolio to show his right-wing credentials by introducing draconian amendments to the Trade Practices Act, which were later repealed. The tough anti-union approach appealed to Fraser, who promoted him to Minister for Special Trade Negotiations and Minister assisting the Prime Minister. At this stage the Prime Minister regarded him as a possible successor, an alternative to the ambitious Andrew Peacock.

The Fraser years were lucky ones for Howard. During the 1977 election campaign the Treasurer, Phillip Lynch, was forced to stand down over a land scandal; Howard, as a clean skin, was the replacement. He took on the economist John Hewson as an adviser and became a zealous free-marketeer. He pressed for a consumption tax, but as was the case with Keating a few years later had the idea rejected by a more cautious Prime Minister. However, he was able to initiate a program of tax reform and used the report of a committee headed by Keith Campbell to take the first steps in the process of financial deregulation.

His day-to-day running of the economy was less successful; stagflation had set in, with high unemployment, inflation running at 12.5 per cent, and interest rates peaking at a horrific 21 per cent. Nonetheless his advancement continued; in 1982, after Peacock unsuccessfully challenged Fraser for the party leadership, Howard replaced Lynch as deputy leader. For a brief period he seemed to be the heir apparent.

But by the time Fraser lost the 1983 election, he had become reconciled with Peacock and had turned firmly against Howard. Later he said it was Howard's attitude to race which he found unacceptable; alone among his ministers Howard had opposed the admission of Vietnamese refugees and had spoken against Australia applying trade sanctions to the apartheid regime in South Africa. Peacock easily beat Howard for the leadership, but Howard remained as deputy. The ongoing feud between the two was to bedevil the Liberal Party for the next decade.

When Peacock was re-endorsed as leader after a strong but unsuccessful campaign against Bob Hawke in the 1984 election, he demanded a pledge of loyalty from Howard; Howard refused, asserting his right as a member of the party to stand for the leadership if and when he chose. After a year of undermining by his deputy, Peacock brought things to a head; he asked the party to replace Howard with a deputy of his own choosing. But the Liberals insisted on confirming both men in their respective jobs. Peacock took the result as a vote of no confidence and resigned, leaving Howard to step into the leadership.

He was clearly not ready for it. He failed to unite the party or to capitalise on the economic downturn brought on by a sharp fall in the Australian dollar and the temporary loss of Australia's AAA credit rating. Indeed, he unwisely said, "The times will suit me," which was interpreted as being callous and selfish. And any remaining chance of victory in the 1987 election was swept away when the populist but ultimately grotesque Premier of Queensland, Joh Bjelke-Petersen, announced he would run his own campaign to become Prime Minister. "We'll have trouble with that lunatic now," Howard muttered gloomily to Janette when they heard the news, and so it proved. The conservative vote fragmented and Hawke was returned comfortably.

In 1988 Howard tried to improve his public image by spelling out a social agenda, but this too went wrong. He opposed multiculturalism, wanted to slow the rate of Asian immigration and rejected calls for a pact of reconciliation with indigenous Australia. In a party room still made up largely of survivors from the more liberal Fraser era, it was a big step backwards. The Peacock supporters regrouped, and in 1989 once again had the numbers. Howard mused, "I won the leadership by accident and I lost it by ambush," and, borrowing a line from Labor's Bill Hayden, added that to become leader again he would need to become Lazarus with a triple bypass.

But he didn't give up; after losing again in 1990 Peacock was replaced by Howard's old adviser John Hewson and Howard reversed their previous roles by becoming Hewson's spokesman for Industrial Relations. He had a radical anti-union agenda, which became part of Hewson's Fightback! package, and campaigned vigorously in what was seen to be an unlosable election for Hewson; however, when Hewson lost in 1993, Howard immediately challenged him for the leadership. Although Hewson was now clearly a lame duck, the party still preferred him to Howard; and when Hewson was eventually dumped, his replacement was not Howard but the ridiculous Alexander Downer.

A less stubborn man would have taken that as the ultimate humiliation and resigned. Howard persevered and, after a succession of gaffes by Downer, finally returned to the leadership in 1995 with the backing of Downer's deputy, Peter Costello, who retained the position under Howard.

A favourite line of Howard's was that people knew what he stood for; but in the 1996 election about all they knew was that he had promised there would never, ever be a GST, that he wanted to make them relaxed and comfortable, and that he wasn't Paul Keating. That was enough; Howard won a record majority and immediately appropriated the luxurious harbourside property Kirribilli House in Sydney as the residence for himself and his family rather than the more humble Lodge in Canberra. To the victor, the spoils.

He followed through with the most ruthless purge of the public service in its history: no less than a third of all permanent heads were axed, to be replaced with others considered more amenable. To reinforce the message Howard instructed his ministers that when they were making appointments, a sympathy with government policies should not be seen as a disadvantage. Another politician he greatly admired, Margaret Thatcher, once told him that the key to government was to make sure the sixty people who really run the country are your own troops. Howard was taking the advice and he extended it to the party room, where he began a purge of moderate members. In all but its name, the Liberal Party was to be cleansed of liberalism.

His first year in office was a tumultuous one. He had promised to implement a strict code of ministerial conduct; as a result he was forced to sack several junior ministers for relatively minor offences. After that the code fell into abeyance and far more serious transgressions were left unpunished. Then a madman massacred thirty-five people at Port Arthur in Tasmania. As a result Howard introduced laws on gun control, a move that was overwhelmingly popular; it was applauded by well over 90 per cent of the population.

And then there was Pauline Hanson, a Queenslander who had been disendorsed by the Liberal Party after making what were considered to be anti-Aboriginal comments. She was elected nonetheless and her maiden speech was far more inflammatory, including the line that Australia was in danger of being swamped by Asians. Most of Howard's colleagues demanded that he denounce the speech, but the Prime Minister temporised, talking instead about lifting the pall of censorship imposed by advocates of political correctness. It was the start of his war with those he called the elites, by which he meant not the rich and powerful, but leftist intellectuals – indeed, just about anyone who disagreed with him.

With the wiping out of the budget deficit, the first year went pretty well – so well that at the start of 1997 Howard felt strong enough to break his biggest promise and re-open the campaign for a consumption tax. In the process he appropriated vast sums of money for an unprecedented political advertising campaign. In the past government advertising had sometimes been partisan, but at least it had been confined to changes which had passed into law; the GST campaign was about legislation which had not even been drafted, let alone enacted. It was simply Liberal Party policy. Some lawyers believed the expenditure was verging on actual corruption.

By this time voters were starting to wonder if they did, indeed, know what Howard stood for: the mild-mannered conservative for whom they had voted was turning into a right-wing iconoclast before their very eyes. The impression was reinforced by Howard's conduct of a prolonged dispute on the waterfront, during which the government appeared to collude with employers in tactics which were always dubious and at one stage found to be illegal.

And then there was Howard's approach to Aboriginal Australia. Instead of continuing the previous government's moves towards reconciliation, Howard appeared bent on picking fights. When a report from a commission headed by Sir Ronald Wilson revealed the horrors stemming from previous policies of child removal, Howard not only refused to apologise but also launched a personal attack on the author. When the High Court brought down its Wik judgement, which found that Aboriginal land tenure could still exist on some private leaseholds, Howard refused to negotiate and suspended the Racial Discrimination Act to bring in legislation to nullify the court's decision. Pauline Hanson applauded, but many Australians, including some in his own party, were uneasy.

Even so, the government scraped back at the 1998 election, albeit on less than half of the popular vote, and a watered-down version of the GST was eventually passed with the help of the Democrats; it became the Howard government's only substantial claim to economic reform, although he and Peter Costello did tighten the banking regulations and formalise the independence of the Reserve Bank.

Domestically, 1999 was memorable for the debate and referendum on making Australia a republic; Howard had inherited the commitment but was adamantly opposed to change, saying publicly that Australia would become a republic over his dead body. In the process that followed he effortlessly outmanoeuvred the republicans led by his fellow Liberal Malcolm Turnbull, who declared that Howard had broken the nation's heart. The major international event was the strife in East Timor; Australia had been instrumental in persuading Indonesia to hold a referendum on the state's independence and was later involved in the international military effort to contain the violence that followed.

But the voters were not impressed and within the government itself there were tensions triggered by Peter Costello's expectation that Howard would step down from the leadership and give him his turn. By the start of 2001 the polls were predicting a disastrous election for Howard, and a series of by-election defeats forced a series of radical policy shifts. The government had previously been reasonably thrifty; now it became profligate and by the end of a winter of pork barrelling things were looking up.

Then came the *Tampa* affair: a group of asylum seekers whose boat was sinking was rescued by a Norwegian freighter, but Howard refused them permission to land in Australia. Howard appealed to the nationalism and xenophobia of the electorate with the pronouncement: "We will decide who comes to Australia and the circumstances under which they come." The navy was ordered to turn the *Tampa* away from Australian waters and the asylum seekers were removed to camps hastily set up in Nauru and Papua New Guinea in what was called the Pacific Solution. Intolerance and bigotry were fanned by government claims, later shown to be false, that some asylum seekers had thrown their children overboard.

And in the midst of the furore Howard visited the United States and was fortuitously in Washington on September 11 to personally pledge Australia's support for George W. Bush's war on terror. The election that followed was a foregone conclusion, with voters emerging from the booths making remarks like "I went for Johnny Howard because he knows how to deal with the towel heads." Authors David Marr and Marian Wilkinson christened it Howard's "Dark Victory".

Certainly it seemed to hamstring him in his third term; the government appeared to have run out of both policies and puff. Howard's popularity was on the wane and for some months in 2004 Labor's new and idiosyncratic leader Mark Latham held a clear ascendancy in the polls. In the end he proved too flaky for the electorate, but the warning signs were there. None of Howard's four wins could be put down to his own popularity. In 1996 commentator Malcolm McGregor put the view that Howard won only because he was running against Paul Keating; if he had been unopposed, he would have lost. In 1998 Labor won the two-party-preferred vote, but unfortunately for Kim Beazley the popular vote did not translate into seats in parliament. 2001 was the dark victory, and in 2004 Howard was again saved by Labor fielding an unelectable candidate. By 2007 he had been in power for eleven years and the "It's Time" factor was well and truly in play.

Howard, having unexpectedly gained control of the Senate in 2004, decided on one last big gamble. With no mandate and no consultation with his colleagues he introduced WorkChoices, an industrial relations package which went far beyond what would normally be called reasonable. Paul Keating had introduced enterprise bargaining, by which individual businesses could negotiate with their workforces rather than having to comply with industry-wide deals; Howard now proposed a system whereby employers could offer individual employees take-it-or-leave-it contracts with no intervention by the unions or anyone else. It pushed the balance too far; the union movement ran an effective campaign to counter the flood of taxpayer-funded government advertising and it was clear by the end of 2006 that all Labor needed to do to win was to produce a credible leader. In December they did so with Kevin Rudd, who promptly swept to an unassailable lead over Howard in the opinion polls.

Howard changed tack with a dramatic intervention into Aboriginal communities in the Northern Territory, but the majority of voters remained unimpressed. There was just one chance left: a switch to Costello who, it was now revealed, had been promised the job by Howard after the 1998 election and had suffered in silence ever since. Howard had always said he would leave the leadership when his colleagues asked him; with the election looming, a majority of his ministers did just that. But Howard once again reneged and Costello still refused to issue a direct challenge. On 24 November 2007 John Howard lost not only government but also his own seat, becoming the first Prime Minister since Stanley Bruce to do so.

It had been a long run: thirty-four years in parliament, with eleven of them as Prime Minister, a record beaten only by Menzies. In the end there was not much to show for it. His last two terms in particular were notably unproductive apart from WorkChoices, whose brief life was quickly terminated by the new Labor government. From the first two terms, only the GST survives as a serious piece of legislation. Yet if the Howard years changed little in the law, they had a huge effect on the culture. Most Australians certainly became wealthier, but in the process they became more materialistic and self-centred. Howard constantly held up the ideal of mateship, but in practice he was much more concerned with individuals taking responsibility for themselves than in fostering genuine co-operation within communities, let alone in a wider international context. Indeed, much of his political success derived from setting groups against each other, from bolstering fear and loathing.

Those he derided as the elites satirised his fondness for the white picket fence, the simple joys of the cricket field and the 1950s music of Buddy Holly, but these were the genuine expressions of a man who always looked a little out of place as a leader in twenty-first century Australia. But he knew how to relate to people; they may not have loved him, but for a long time they voted for him. And they even bought his memoirs; incredibly, *Lazarus Rising* became a bestseller. But how many actually read it, and how many felt truly relaxed and comfortable during that divisive decade, remains another question.

KEVIN MICHAEL **RUDD**

It was Arthur Fadden who gave the terse description of political life: "A rooster one day, a feather duster the next." He was presumably recalling his own brief time at the top.

But the scenario applies even more to Kevin Rudd. Shortly after his election in 2007 Rudd soared to positively Hawke-like heights of popularity; according to the polls he was Labor's new Messiah. But less than three years later the same polls had plunged to such an extent that some party warlords did not believe he could win a second election and denied him the right to even try: Rudd became the only Prime Minister to be sacked by his own party in his first term of office, although two others (Menzies and Gorton) were dumped after contesting and winning a single election. And then, a little over a year later, his popularity had recovered to the extent that the opinion polls indicated that Labor's only hope of survival was to reinstate him. No other leader in Australian history has hit such peaks and troughs in so short a period.

Kevin Michael Rudd hardly fitted the daredevil mould. He was born in 1957 near Eumundi, a village in south-east Queensland, where his convict-descended father Bert worked as a sharefarmer. Young Kevin was a sickly child, contracting rheumatic fever which caused him permanent heart damage; nonetheless he enjoyed his rural childhood until, when he was eleven, his father died after botched medical treatment and the family had to leave the farm.

The exact circumstances of the eviction are disputed, but there is no doubt they had a traumatic effect on the child, which was compounded when he was sent to board at the Marist Brothers' school at Ashgrove in Brisbane as a charity case. He found the place harsh and class-bound, and relief came only when his mother Margaret retrained as a nurse and moved the family to Nambour. Rudd thrived at the state high school, graduating as dux and winning a state oratory award on the way through. He also attended ALP meetings, although his father had been a staunch Country Party supporter. A fellow student was the man who was to become first his political rival and then his Treasurer, Wayne Swan.

Rudd was accepted at the Australian National University in Canberra, where he subsisted by cleaning the residence of political journalist Laurie Oakes and studied Arts, specialising in Asian Studies. He also joined the Student Christian Movement, meeting a fellow believer, Thérèse Rein. He graduated with first-class honours and was rewarded with a stint in Taiwan, where he honed his language skills. On his return he married Thérèse and joined the Department of Foreign Affairs, which took note of his expertise on Asia by posting him to Stockholm. He was later moved to Beijing, where his fellow diplomats found him uppity and hard to get on with.

In 1988 he resigned from the department to join the then Queensland opposition leader, Wayne Goss, as his chief of staff. Goss became premier the following year and Rudd became an immensely powerful, but generally unpopular, figure in the state government. In 1992 Goss appointed him as the first director-general of the cabinet office, effectively making him the state's bureaucratic dictator. He was respected for his many skills and tireless work ethic, but was disliked and feared for what was seen as his arrogance and failure to acknowledge that he was part of a team. There were few mourners when he took sick leave for heart surgery.

When the Goss government fell, Rudd took a job with the accounting firm KPMG, but his mind was now set on politics. He contested the federal seat of Griffith in 1996 and lost, but won it in 1998. In caucus he was regarded as an up-and-comer, but once again his sense of superiority made enemies, especially among those who knew of his reputation from his Queensland days. However, in 2001 his talent and diligence saw him promoted to the frontbench as shadow Minister for Foreign Affairs. Like his leader, Kim Beazley, he was regarded as strongly pro-American, too much so for Mark Latham, who became leader in 2003. To ensure stability Latham retained him in the job, but the two clashed repeatedly.

When Latham lost in 2004, Beazley came back as leader with Rudd's support, but Rudd was positioning himself as the natural successor should his leader falter. And when the scandal broke over the Australian Wheat Board paying bribes to the Iraqi government to secure contracts, it was Rudd who led the charge against the government and did considerable, though not terminal, damage. He was now seen as having surpassed his contemporary rivals Wayne Swan and Stephen Smith from the right of the party in the race to the top. But he was still far short of the numbers to mount a challenge.

This changed at the end of 2006, when Rudd entered an improbable partnership with Julia Gillard, the doyen of the left. The left, always the minority faction, could not make Gillard leader, but by throwing their weight behind one or other side of a right split between Rudd and Beazley they could get her up as deputy and perhaps heir apparent. In a tense caucus meeting, the odd couple won by 49–39. It was a hugely successful strategy. Throughout 2007 John Howard floundered against the Labor revival and Rudd, while still mistrusted by many in caucus, became something of a cult figure with the general public. He became a contributor to serious magazines with essays on religion and politics. At the other end of the scale he was a regular on daytime television and FM radio and a prominent presence online. And when the election came around, he swept to victory under the pop logo "Kevin '07". But he was still relatively unknown to the general public. He was clearly a nerd and a God-botherer, and was inordinately fond of asking himself rhetorical questions. And he talked in cliches; there were constant references to a fork in the road and a bridge too far. His apparent devotion to sport seemed even more hollow than that of his rival John Howard. He was not the kind of politician to whom Australian voters could relate; hence the rather self-conscious development of the media personality. One cartoonist drew him as the comic strip boy-hero Tintin and another as a toy balloon.

But it was not all froth and bubble. Rudd promised an education revolution and a national broadband network to position Australia in the modern world, along with a number of bread-and-butter reforms such as the abolition of the hated WorkChoices. But it was the symbolic issues which resonated with the public. Howard had consistently refused to sign and ratify the Kyoto protocol on climate change or to apologise to the generation of indigenous Australians forcibly removed from their families. Rudd did both and his popularity soared to undreamt-of levels. But that was as good as it got; the Global Financial Crisis struck and while the Australian economy escaped almost unscathed, the government was seriously affected.

Rudd, on Treasury advice, put together a large and urgent stimulus package which included instant cash handouts to families and massive infrastructure projects. To achieve their purpose these had to be rushed into place, which meant that in some cases, notably a program to insulate homes and a program for new school buildings, they were inadequately supervised and consequently rorted by unscrupulous tradesmen enticed by the prospect of easy money. The opposition and its media supporters mounted a sustained campaign against what it claimed were wasted taxpayer resources and the public responded. The government received little if any credit for saving Australia from joining the rest of the industrialised world in recession and financial turmoil, but was blamed for its extravagance.

And the slide continued: Rudd and the opposition leader, Malcolm Turnbull, basically agreed on the need for action on climate change and between them had hammered out legislation to put in place an emissions trading scheme. But sceptics and conservatives within the Liberal Party staged a revolt and Turnbull was dumped in favour of Tony Abbott, who flatly refused to endorse the arrangement. Rudd was tempted to call a double dissolution election over the issue, but decided against it and was persuaded by his more cautious advisers, led by Gillard and Swan, to put the legislation to one side. The effect was immediate and lethal. Rudd had once called climate change the great political, moral and economic challenge of our times; he had made speeches that sounded very like sermons and set it up as an absolute priority for Australia and the world. Now, apparently, it was just another disposable policy.

Rudd was already in trouble on other fronts; his proposal for a tax on the super-profits miners were making from the commodities boom was opposed in a ferocious advertising campaign from the miners, and discussions had become messy and bogged down. And asylum seekers were once again coming to Australia: Rudd was blamed for repealing the most brutal aspects of John Howard's Pacific Solution. His standing in the polls plummeted, and Rudd's many enemies in the party pounced. He had never commanded solid factional support, and had made few real friends: many in the party felt they had been treated with contempt, both by Rudd himself and by his brash young staff members. He had taken on the role of a one-man band, an autocrat – not a true Labor leader.

Rudd's ability to hold an election-winning lead in the polls was his only real asset. With that disappearing, the knives came out. Julia Gillard had been impeccably loyal for two and a half years, but now the faction bosses offered her the leadership on a plate, and she took it. Rudd wanted to fight, but the numbers were already locked up, so he resigned, although not without protest. And he made it clear that he was not going anywhere; he remained available, indeed eager, to serve as part of the new government. Gillard left him on the backbench until she called an early election, but some backbenchers appealed for his help in holding marginal seats, particularly in Queensland, where he was seen as something of a martyred local boy. And in the hung parliament that followed, Gillard had to accommodate him; had he left the parliament, her government would almost certainly have fallen.

The obvious, indeed probably the only, spot for the former diplomat was Foreign Affairs; even as Prime Minister it had been his chief area of interest and achievement. He had played a leading role in expanding the G8 group of rich nations to the far more representative G20, on which Australia held a seat, reinstated the United Nations as a major consideration in Australian policy and, most notably, recalled Australian troops from Iraq. And there was much unfinished business, including Australia's bid for a seat on the UN security council. Gillard gave him the job, no doubt hoping that he would use it to spend as much time out of Australia as possible; and he certainly seemed to be trying. A period in hospital for further heart surgery also kept him out of parliament.

But as Gillard's own popularity fell to unprecedented depths, Rudd's rose; by the spring of 2011 he was once again by far the most popular Labor politician – among the public, that is; the warlords who had sacked him and many others in the caucus swore they would rather gnaw off their own limbs than have him back. It was a tense and uncomfortable situation, particularly for Gillard. Rudd continued to protest his loyalty, but he would not have been human if he had not felt at least a frisson of satisfaction at the discomfiture of his supplanter.

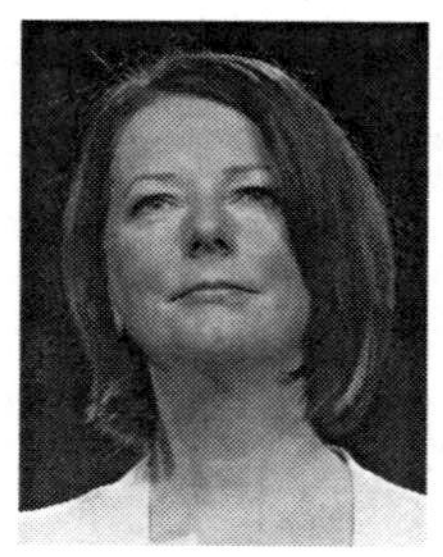

JULIA EILEEN GILLARD

JULIA GILLARD WAS not Australia's first red-haired Prime Minister; the title belongs to James Scullin. She was not even Australia's first Welsh Prime Minister; Billy Hughes, though born in London, would indignantly claim that honour.

But she was unquestionably our first unmarried Prime Minister, and more significantly, our first female Prime Minister. And as such much – too much – was expected of her. To justify the fact that she had deposed the previous leader she had not only to prove herself more capable than he had been, but also to do it in a way that brought glory and credit to her gender.

ALP state politics had a sad record of women thrust into the leadership when things became desperate, whose role was simply to cushion the inevitable loss: Joan Kirner, Carmen Lawrence, Kristina Keneally. But there had also been some successes: Clare Martin and Anna Bligh. Now the sisterhood had moved into the federal arena, and Gillard was the guinea pig. It was not a role she had sought or relished, but like the prime ministership itself, it was an offer she could not refuse.

Julia Eileen Gillard was born in 1961 in Barry, Wales, a small town in a district known locally as The Valley of the Witch – a coincidence which delighted her political opponents. In her childhood she suffered from bronchopneumonia and the doctors suggested a move to a warmer and drier climate, so at the age of five Julia and her family ended up in Adelaide. Her father worked as a psychiatric nurse and her mother cooked for the Salvation Army; Julia and her elder sister, Alison, sometimes helped to prepare the meals.

Gillard was educated at the Mitcham Demonstration School and later at Unley High, where she is remembered as an enthusiastic debater. She enrolled in the Arts faculty at the University of Adelaide but soon moved to Melbourne where she threw herself into student politics. She became secretary of the Socialist Forum but was never a true radical; in fact she became part of a group formed to wrest control of the Australian Union of Students from the Maoists and Trotskyists and as its president campaigned on local student welfare issues rather than the revolutionary international programs of her predecessors. At the time her political hero was the Welsh socialist Aneurin Bevan.

Gillard graduated with degrees in Arts and Law in 1986 and took a job with the Melbourne legal firm of Slater and Gordon, where she specialised in industrial and employment cases; she was made a partner in 1990. Six years later she left to join the staff of the Labor opposition leader in Victoria, John Brumby, where as his chief of staff she helped to set up Emily's List, a group dedicated to ensuring women were preselected for winnable seats in parliament. She joined the

ALP's socialist left faction, but was regarded by some old hands as something of an opportunist; Kim Carr and Lindsay Tanner both believed that she was more interested in gaining preselection than in policy and ideology. If so, it worked; in 1998 she was rewarded with the safe seat of Lalor, which she won comfortably.

She was immediately seen as a promising talent and in 2001 joined the frontbench with the shadow portfolio of Population and Immigration, to be augmented by Indigenous Affairs two years later. She supported Simon Crean as leader, and then switched her allegiance to Mark Latham who, ignoring her membership of the left faction, gave her the important responsibility of Health, pitting her against the then minister Tony Abbott; the clashes between the two became an eagerly anticipated part of the parliamentary theatre. At the 2004 election she embraced a policy of free medical and hospital care for seniors, which was popular with many voters but was regarded as impractical by the hard heads.

Following the election loss and the resignation of Latham, Gillard was seen as a prospect for the deputy leadership of the party, but she was unwilling to challenge her fellow lefty Jenny Macklin. Nonetheless by 2006 the polls rated her Labor's most popular politician, ahead of the leader, Kim Beazley, and his principal challenger, Kevin Rudd. She soon formed an alliance with Rudd; as a member of the left she had to be content with the deputy's job, but she brought more votes to their successful challenge than Rudd did. He refused her the role of shadow Treasurer but she took over the key area of Industrial Relations to oppose the Howard government's WorkChoices program; in government she added Education to her responsibilities.

In the lead-up to the 2007 election and for two and a half years after it, the partnership worked well; Gillard proved competent and loyal, apparently content to wait her turn. She was seen by all, including the dominant right faction, as the logical successor to Rudd and it was assumed that she would take over the leadership sometime in Rudd's second or third term as Prime Minister. But in 2010 a series of miscalculations saw Rudd's popularity and Labor's vote slipping alarmingly. Rudd's arrogant behaviour had alienated the factional bosses of the right to the extent that they were ready to move for a change. Gillard was reluctant, but when one of Rudd's staff members was found to be surreptitiously querying caucus members about her loyalty, she agreed to run, and was installed unopposed as ALP leader and consequently Prime Minister.

She justified the coup by saying that a good government had lost its way, and promised to settle three nagging issues: climate change policy, the row over Labor's plan for a new tax on mining super-profits, and the problem of the increasing numbers of asylum seekers arriving in boats from Indonesia. But she was unable to provide the quick fixes needed, and instead called an early election for which neither she nor the opposition leader Tony Abbott was prepared. The result was a slogan-driven and lacklustre campaign which resulted in a hung parliament: Labor and the coalition controlled 72 seats each, with the remaining six going to independents or minor parties. After lengthy negotiations Gillard secured the conditional support of four of them and was able to form a government, but at a heavy price.

Those holding the balance of power made demands which were to prove very difficult for her government to deliver and to cost it significant support. The Greens member Adam

Bandt demanded that Gillard introduce a carbon tax, something she had specifically ruled out during the election campaign. She had maintained support for some kind of emissions trading scheme, but not for a direct tax. For Abbott and the opposition this was an unforgivable broken promise, one that made her unfit to govern, and his ferocious campaign against it attracted considerable public support. The Tasmanian Andrew Wilkie demanded legislation to restrict the use of poker machines by problem gamblers; the government faced vigorous and well-funded resistance from the clubs and pubs before the legislation was even drafted. The rural independents Tony Windsor and Rob Oakeshott were less specific but insisted on having input into every facet of government, leaving voters with the impression that Gillard and her ministers were incapable of implementing Labor's own platform.

In the circumstances Gillard did surprisingly well in simply maintaining a stable administration; bills were passed and progress made on most of the ongoing programs she had inherited from Rudd. But the three key issues she had nominated proved very difficult. Legislation for a carbon tax acceptable to all four of her supportive independents was eventually produced, and would take effect in July 2012, nearly a year and a half before an election was due; the hope was that Abbott's scare campaign would then be shown to be spurious, but it would be a long wait to find out. And even a watered-down version of the mining super-profits tax stalled in negotiations, with the threat of a revived advertising campaign from the miners hanging over the government.

But it was the problem of asylum seekers that proved the most intractable. Gillard's first attempt at a solution involved the establishment of a regional processing centre in East

Timor, but the Timorese government, after some bickering, refused to agree. She then proposed a deal with Malaysia by which that country would accept some 800 unprocessed boat people and in exchange Australia would take 4000 bona-fide refugees. Malaysia was willing, but the deal was struck down by the Australian High Court. To pass legislation required to get around the court's decision Gillard was forced to rely on the votes of the coalition, which insisted that its own Pacific Solution – which Rudd had overturned as brutal and unnecessary – was in fact more humane than the Malaysia Solution. The bills were rejected and the problem remained unsolved.

Throughout this process Labor's support plummeted; by the spring of 2011 the party's primary vote was mired catastrophically in the mid-twenties and Gillard herself was well on the way to beating Paul Keating's record as Australia's most unpopular Prime Minister. Her television performances were studied and wooden and her broad Australian accent, once something of an asset within the Labor movement, was now seen as grating. On a personal level she could still be persuasive, charming and funny, but this side of her – the real Julia she had promised to reveal during the election campaign – was not the one the voters saw. Even within the party there was wide discontent; many had never forgiven her for the way she deposed Rudd, and those in her former left faction felt betrayed by many of her policies, including her personal opposition to same-sex marriage: given that she was openly in a de facto relationship, they regarded her zealous support for traditional marriage as inconsistent and hypocritical. And despite her obvious toughness, she was not being taken altogether seriously: the

ABC ran a short comedy called *At Home With Julia*, parodying the domestic existence of Gillard and her partner, a hairdresser named Tim Mathieson. It was widely regarded as unfunny and disrespectful, but very few voters rushed to defend their Prime Minister.

As parliament wound up for the year, there seemed little prospect of a second election win for our twenty-seventh Prime Minister. The only comfort for Julia Gillard, and indeed for the Labor Party, was that there was also little enthusiasm for installing Tony Abbott, the erratic opposition leader, as our twenty-eighth. If Gillard, for all her skill and persistence, had often appeared out of her depth in the job, it seemed unlikely that Abbott, best known for participating in sporting events clad in Speedos or lycra and derided by his many enemies as the Mad Monk, would be able to master it.

But then, perhaps no one could. In 110 years, the role of the Prime Minister has become vastly more complex; technology, globalisation and the demands of a better educated, more ambitious and less forgiving electorate have combined to make the position one requiring a range of skills unimaginable to Edmund Barton and his fellow federationists.

More complex, certainly – but more challenging? The pioneers who welded the brawling colonies of the nineteenth century into the extraordinary structure that is Australia had much to be proud of – and we have much to thank them, and all their successors, for. It is to those twenty-six men and one woman that this book is gratefully dedicated.

NOTE ON SOURCES

For the basic facts on the careers of the prime ministers I have relied largely on *The Australian Dictionary of Biography*, *Australian Prime Ministers* edited by Michelle Grattan and the earlier *Mr Prime Minister* by Colin Hughes. The fleshing out comes from numerous other publications, news reports and anecdotes; these were used more extensively when considering the later prime ministers and almost exclusively in the case of the last three. The value judgements and comments are, of course, my own except where otherwise indicated.

I should also acknowledge the help and encouragement from all the good people at Black Inc., especially my publisher, Chris Feik, and my editor, Nikola Lusk. And as always, the love and support of my partner, Jenny.

Mungo MacCallum
November 2011

Photos (cover): Malcolm Fraser: National Archives of Australia (NAA): A6180, 6/5/77/12. Julia Gillard © Troy Constable. Bob Hawke: NAA: A6180, 31/5/83/2. John Howard: US Navy photo/Mass Communication Specialist 2nd Class Jarod Hodge (released). Paul Keating © Newspix/News Limited. Gough Whitlam © Newspix/Nathan Edwards. All used with permission.

Photos (internals): Malcolm Fraser: NAA: A6180, 6/1/78/2. John Gorton: NAA: A1200, L63640A. Bob Hawke: NAA: A6180, 31/5/83/2. Harold Holt: NAA: A1200, L52058. John Howard: NAA: A8746, KN6/3/96/12. Paul Keating: NAA: A6180, 10/11/95/1. John McEwen: NAA: A1200, L66448. William McMahon: NAA: A1200, L55189. Gough Whitlam © Australian Information Services. Source: National Library of Australia. All used with permission.

CPSIA information can be obtained at www.ICGtesting.com
Printed in the USA
LVOW092319120412

277443LV00002B/11/P

9 781863 955539